THE CENTERS OF CIVILIZATION SERIES

ALGIERS

IN THE AGE OF THE

CORSAIRS

Algiers

in the Age of the Corsairs

by WILLIAM SPENCER

UNIVERSITY OF OKLAHOMA PRESS : NORMAN

Library of Congress Cataloging in Publication Data

Spencer, William.
    Algiers in the age of the corsairs.

    (The Centers of civilization series)
    Bibliography: p. 177
    Includes index.
    1. Algiers (City)—History. I. Title. II. Series.
DT299.A5S67   965'.3   75-38728
ISBN: 0-8061-1334-0

Copyright 1976 by the University of Oklahoma Press, Pub-
lishing Division of the University. Composed and printed at
Norman, Oklahoma, U.S.A., by the University of Oklahoma
Press. First edition.

FOREWORD

The story of Algiers is one of the great paradoxes in the annals of Mediterranean civilization. Algiers' urban origins are obscure, and its rank among both classical and Islamic cities remained insignificant throughout the periods of Roman, Byzantine, Vandal, and Arab domination of the southern shores of the "Great Sea." Yet a thousand years of anonymity ended abruptly as the city developed in the sixteenth and seventeenth centuries into the dominant maritime power of the western Mediterranean region. Not only was Algiers more dreaded by Christian nations and peoples than its nominal superior, the Ottoman Porte, but also it continued to inspire an aura of awe and dread during the long decline of Ottoman power. As the capital of a stable, well-established

North African state, Algiers along with Tunis and Tripoli represented the cutting edge of Ottoman Islamic power engaged in the counter crusade against Christianity, a whetted blade thrust deep into Christian territory.

One element in Algiers' meteoric rise to prominence resulted from the policy decision on the part of the Ottomans to advance their interests against their Christian foes through the use of African land bases. The Ottomans, unlike their Muslim Arab and Berber predecessors who had launched campaigns from these same land bases against the infidel, were not primarily interested in the acquisition of Christian territory on the opposite shores of the Mediterranean. The Ottoman commitment involved essentially the recovery of North African ports occupied by the Spanish—parts of the traditional homeland of Islam—and such protecting islands as Djerba, off the coast of Tunisia. Of greater significance in terms of Ottoman grand strategy was the formation of an effective naval arm which would duplicate at sea the systematic success of Ottoman land armies in eastern Europe, thus assuring the domination of the empire over its Christian adversaries. The North African harbors offered the best possibilities for the development of this policy; furthermore they were in Spanish hands and could be made the objects of the jihad (holy war) to which the Ottomans so enthusiastically subscribed.

This Ottoman naval strategy was primarily responsible for the emergence of Algiers as a first-class power. Lacking a maritime heritage or competence in seamanship, the Ottomans utilized their right to acquired leadership in the Islamic world centered in their Padishah as caliph to win the allegiance and services of Muslim sea captains from all parts of the Mediterranean. The ancient and honorable profession of the corsair received legal sanction through the intervention of an article of faith, that of the jihad. Corsairs who had preyed on the shipping of many flags now found themselves restricted, but more than compensated through the pay, facilities, and services and the honor of serving the sultan-caliph. Opportunities to rise through the ranks of the newly created Ottoman fleet were available to all men of competence and daring; the very highest post, that of *Kapudan derya* (admiral of the sea), was within the reach of any corsair captain.

Judged by the observations of both Europeans and the Ottoman officials who dealt with them, the Algerine corsairs were better at their task than any other group. More of their captains reached the highest posts in the fleet, and Ottoman archives detail numerous requests for pay increases and emoluments from the Imperial Treasury for individual corsairs, such requests being invariably honored. The Algerine accomplishment becomes more significant when measured against the Algerine past, the city's tradition being one of modest mercantilism until the expedition of the Barbarossa brothers endowed it with a ready-made corsair establishment.

Yet the role of Algiers in Mediterranean civilization would remain unclear if measured solely in terms of Ottoman foreign policy executed by the corsairs. The Corsair Age, a period of grandeur for Turkish North Africa with the Algerine state as its epitome, vanished as swiftly as it had blossomed. Thus the paradox of Algiers' rise is duplicated by its fall into obscurity. The French soldiers in scarlet cloaks who fulfilled an ancient superstition by their capture of the city by overland assault in 1830 were no more certain than their government of what they had actually accomplished.

But the willingness of other European states to grant France a free hand in northern Africa and the ineptness of Ottoman policy engendered in time the dissociation of *Algeria* from the *Regency of Algiers*.

An efficient and industrious *département* of the *Métropole* replaced the corsair state, which the French labeled as "anarchic" and "irresponsible." Turkish "misgovernment" was widely trumpeted as the root cause for the alleged political and economic backwardness of North Africa. It also became evident that Algiers formed part of the shameful European past when disunited and quarrelsome sovereigns competed for territory and prestige and Algerine corsairs preyed on all. The pleas of the last dey for recognition or assistance went unheeded; he died as an unwanted pensioner of Muhammad Ali. A century after the conquest, the "well-guarded city" of Mediterranean folklore had become a provincial French bourgeois town, its hinterland indistinguishable from other rich agricultural regions of the mother country. In place of the swarms of men from many nations who had thronged the narrow streets of the corsair capital were a few wealthy European visitors escaping the rigors of the northern winter, along with the resident French bourgeoisie.

The enormous effort by which corsair Algiers was converted into French Algeria, along with the total denigration of the Algerine state, however, should not conceal the very real and significant contributions of the Regency to North African development and to its place in Mediterranean civilization. Official documents, primarily French and Ottoman, but supplemented by the reports of other visitors present a different picture of Algiers. Christians and Muslims alike gave the state high marks for its orderliness, stability, respect for law, social cohesion, and cultural attainments. Algiers was well known to citizens of Constantinople as the head-quarters of the most successful arm of the Ottoman fleet. The city served equally well as a center for the introduction of Turkish customs, costumes, and traditions into North Africa. The evidence of archives, of diplomatic correspondence, and of coinage confirm the strong attachment of the Algerine state to the Ottoman Porte. The campaigns of the corsairs brought economic and, indirectly, cultural enrichment to Algiers, yet its basic Turkish structure never changed during its three centuries of existence. The exactions of the Algerines were a constant source of grief and frustration to their European adversaries, but the latter never doubted Algiers' achievements.

Perhaps the key to the grandeur of Algiers in the corsair age lies in the city's special charisma. It projected an image unique in Mediterranean history. A French nobleman, Le Sieur de Gramaye, in 1619 while en route to Constantinople on an official mission, conveys a vivid impression of this charisma seen at the height of Algerine power: "Algier, the Whip of the Christian World, the terror of Europe, Bridle of Italy and Spain, Scourge of the Islands." Europe's inability to reduce Algiers by naval bombardment helped to preserve and broaden the mystique. To European rulers, the heads of the Algerine state were always "Illustrious and Magnificent Lords," their capital "well-guarded" and "the place of everlasting vigil and combat against the infidel."

Algiers' status in the Mediterranean world was merited by its contributions as well as the exploits of the corsairs. Through the medium of Regency government, Ottoman institutions brought stability to North Africa. The flow of Anatolian recruits and the attachment to the Porte introduced many elements of the eclectic Ottoman civilization into the western Mediterranean. Corsair campaigns produced a fusion of Ottoman with native Maghribi (North African) and European styles, social patterns, architecture, crafts, and the like. A regular system of revenue collection, an efficient subsistence agriculture, and a well-established legitimate commerce along with corsair profits brought to the Regency a high standard of living. Its lands, while they never corresponded to the total territory conquered by France and incorporated into French Algeria, were homogeneous, well managed, and formed of an effective and collaborating social mixture—the exact opposite of the situation which prevailed during the one hundred and thirty years of French control.

Finally, Algiers at the apex of its power generated new initiatives in Mediterranean affairs on the part of both European and Ottoman governments. European power alignments were reshaped frequently as a result of the obligation to deal with the three Ottoman regencies on a regular and direct basis. Corsair indifference to the evolution of international law prompted the convocation of the Congress of Aix-la-Chapelle to deal with questions of tribute, ransom, and slavery in the broad sense. In its ability to play off adversaries which would have overwhelmed the Regency had they been able to unite, Algiers provides an excellent example of the effectiveness of this technique when used properly in the international relations of states. The ability of the Regency to defy the law of political averages for so long, it seems clear, shows not only the effectiveness of its charisma but also the strength of its social cohesion. For three centuries, other than the abortive landings of disorganized Spanish militiamen on its beaches, the internal tranquillity of the corsair state remained undisturbed.

WILLIAM SPENCER

Tallahassee, Florida

CONTENTS

ALGIERS

IN THE AGE OF THE

CORSAIRS

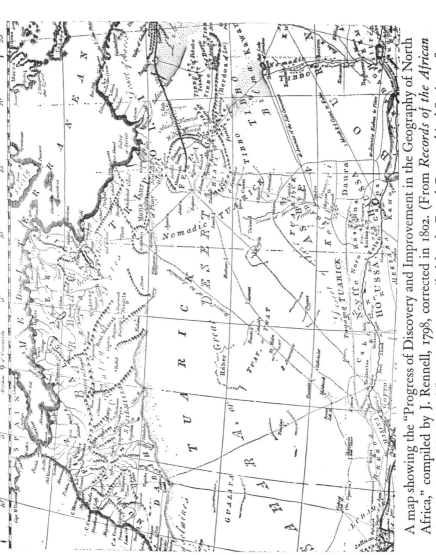

A map showing the "Progress of Discovery and Improvement in the Geography of North Africa," compiled by J. Rennell, 1798, corrected in 1802. (From *Records of the African Association 1788–1831*. The map was compiled for the Royal Geographical Society 1802

FOUNDATIONS OF THE REGENCY

Algiers bloomed late among Mediterranean cities and served a long apprenticeship in maritime commerce before its sudden rise to power. This fact, and a geography which dictated a marine vocation while imposing extreme obstacles to its accomplishment, together probably account for the conflicting legends of the city's origin. Their failure to comprehend its sudden ascendancy in Mediterranean affairs led European chroniclers to invent various mythologies for the foundation of Algiers. The medieval Muslim scholars who dealt with Islamic North Africa rarely mentioned the city, and stressed its Islamic bourgeois nature when they did. The Turks, who set an enduring seal on Algiers with their administrative structure and imported values, dealt in practical matters; evidence of a military ethos or creative social or cultural action on which they might have based their state has been lost to history.

Yet there is a sense of majesty and brooding power gathered about Algiers which was almost certainly there from the beginning, and which required only the appropriate combination of circumstances to activate it toward a manifest destiny. The sailing ship—or contemporary steamer—traversing this inhospitable coast passes mile upon mile of rugged land, rarely broken by the occasional anchorage slashed from the forbidding rocks. Unexpectedly an immense flat bay materializes in the mist, its sheen of waters now ruffled by light winds, now lashed by nor'east squalls, which end just as suddenly as they arise; and at the head of the bay appears the cold gleaming outline of the city, its white buildings seemingly clamped to the steep mountain which rises out of the sea.

Until the arrival of the Turks the chief geographical feature of Algiers was the cluster of small islets which provided a small but safe shelter in their lee from the storms of the open bay. Arab geographers, with their instinct for accurate descriptive labels, named the site Jaza'ir (Cezayir in Turkish), "the islands." The lee shelter permitted a safe anchorage on a firm bottom of sand mixed with mud. The hills which rose from the bay formed a natural amphitheater, difficult of access by land and easily convertible into a strong defensive position for naval warfare. Yet recognition of the potential of Algiers for such activities seems not to have occurred until the arrival of the Turks.

Some sources have identified Algiers with Icosium, a supposed minor link in the North African grain trade to

Rome. Others have called it Carthaginian, on the assumption that the spacing of the Phoenician trading posts a day's sail apart would have made a landfall there logical. However, the nearby ports of Tipasa, Cherchel (Iol), and Dellys, although inferior as anchorages to Algiers, have been identified as parts of the Carthaginian mercantile empire. Furthermore, Icosium is not a Punic word. The difficulty of access to the agricultural hinterland—a *sine qua non* for Phoenician-Punic locations—probably deterred the easterners from establishing a fixed settlement there.

Algiers, or Icosium, was equally unimportant in Roman times, and was bypassed by Numidian Prince Juba in favor of Cherchel when the North African chief, brought up at the Roman court, was granted a fiefdom along the coast. With the establishment by Arab invaders of Islam in the Maghrib, we are on firmer ground. A converted Berber tribe, the Banu Mazghanna, founded a permanent settlement, at the deepest indentation of the bay, which developed into the Kasba and port of Algiers. Local tradition ascribes the destruction of Icosium to the Vandals, during their eastward trek in the fifth century which culminated in the capture of Carthage. In the customary Maghribi fashion, the new settlers combined geography and tribal identity into the first permanent label for the place—al Jaza'ir al-Banu Mazghanna.

Algiers gained its first significance as a result of the contest for temporal power in the Maghrib caused by the rejection by many Berber tribes of the authority of the caliphate. As the Kharijite movement ignited Berber resistance, the possession of urban or coastal strong points became vital. In the tenth century one Bologguin ibn Ziri, a lieutenant of the Fatimid rulers of Ifrikiyya (Tunisia), was entrusted with the government of the central Maghrib, and upon the departure of the Fatimids for Egypt laid claim to authority over the entire region from Kairouan to Tlemcen (Tilimsan). Bologguin fortified and enlarged the three towns of Algiers, Miliana, and Midiyah (Médéa) as a defensive triangle to ensure control over communications and the trade routes between the coast, the Tell, and the steppes. As the rivalry between the Fatimid rulers and the Cordoban caliphs of Spain over hegemony in the western Islamic world intensified, Algiers received its first important vocation. Impregnable to assault by land and difficult of access by sea, it became a sort of eagles' nest perched on the frontier between the two bastions of heterodoxy. The intermittent sieges and assaults which ruined so many other Maghribi cities, and the irruptions of nomad tribes such as the Banu Hilal, hardly ruffled the surface of Algerine life. Even the brilliant Almoravid emir, Yusuf ibn Tashfin, was unable to capture (in 1082) Algiers, although the city surrendered peacefully to his son Ali.

Algiers flourished under Almoravid rule, and was one of the cities chosen for the architectural devotion to the Maliki rite of Islam expressed in the public buildings of the Almoravid emirs. The Almoravid style is clearly recognizable in the Great Mosque with its prayer hall of eleven naves of five bays each, despite the modifications of the Turks.

The vicissitudes which followed Almoravid and Almohad unification of the western Maghrib seem not to have greatly affected the trading vocation of Algiers. Already in 1068 the geographer al-Bakri had observed that "its port, well-protected, was much frequented by sailors from Ifrikiyya and Spain," indicating that a vigorous coastwise traffic existed along with intercourse between the transmarine portions of western Islam. Al-Idrisi, a century later, described Algiers as "a well-populated place, with a flourishing commerce and crowded bazaars; the city is a mountain-girt plain, inhabited by Berber tribes that cultivate wheat, barley, and raise animals and bees."

With the breakup of the Almohad "empire," Algiers came under the nominal authority of various local governors who had been entrusted with Almohad fiefs and subsequently proclaimed their independence. From time to time it was subject to the rulers of Tlemcen, Bujaiyah (Bougie), and Bona, equally acknowledging the Hafsids in Tunis or the Marinid emirs of Morocco as the fortunes of power shifted across the Maghrib. The late twelfth-century uprising (1184–1205) of Almoravids led by the Banu Ghaniya against the Almohads contains one of the rare references to the part played by the city in these struggles. Ali ibn Ghaniya, with the support of disaffected pro-Almoravid tribesmen, established a short-lived Almoravid state based on the former Zirid triangle of Algiers, Miliana, and Midiyah. The lands of the Banu Ghaniya included the Balearic Islands, and although these islands passed into the hands of the Christian King Jaime II of Aragon in 1229, trade between the central Maghrib and the expanded Aragonese state remained vigorous.

In the early part of the fourteenth century a rough balance of forces was achieved in the western Maghrib through the stabilization of three city-state dynasties: the Marinids of Fez, the Ziyanids of Tlemcen, and the Hafsids of Tunis. Algiers, situated at the frontiers of the latter two but not easily controllable by either, managed to establish over a

7

period of time an autonomy based on local government by its merchant oligarchy. It was neither as successful commercially as Tunis nor as prominent culturally as Tlemcen. Yet it was an important port of call for ships from all parts of the Mediterranean and shared in the profits of maritime trade. Catalan records for the period tell us, for example, that between 1308 and 1331 forty-one ships from Aragonese ports alone dropped anchor in the lee of the islands of Algiers.

Commercial relations between the Christian trading states of Europe and the Muslim seaports of the Maghrib prior to the Turkish conquest were controlled by well-established customary laws. Until the advent of formalized corsair warfare in the sixteenth century, breaches of these arrangements were few in number, although an unarmed merchant vessel in the Mediterranean always ran a certain risk from lawless brigands. European vessels were generally accorded free entry into the principal Maghribi ports as far as Tripoli. They had the right to the purchase of provisions, water, and supplies; to protection from local officials in case of disturbances (such as forcible boarding); and at all times to take shelter from sudden storms in the North African anchorages.

Trade between the Maghrib and Europe was most active in the ports where Muslim customs bureaux were located. These bureaux not only supervised and facilitated exchanges but also protected the merchandise and persons of European merchants from the violence of an unruly population. Maghribi customs agents looked after the Christian goods deposited in sealed warehouses called *funduqs*, and Maghribi porters hauled these goods to the appropriate markets for sale, once they had cleared customs. The system enabled the visiting vessels to complete their business in any given port within a short time, often several days, while European shipowners, confident in the reliability of the Maghribi agents, gradually enlarged their warehouses to provide living quarters and offices for their local representatives or agents. In this fashion the European consular service in North Africa came into existence.

Algiers, perhaps due to its rather exposed anchorage or more likely because sovereignty over it was so disputed between the Hafsid emirs and their neighbors, seems not to have been one of the principal customs ports, which were Oran, Bougie, Bona, Tunis, Sfax, Mahdia, Jerba (Djerba), Gabès, and Tripoli. However, as a second-rank port it subscribed to the same well-regulated procedure that applied to Christian ships trading with the Maghrib. Upon arrival at a port the merchandise was unloaded, brought to the customs area, registered to the account of the owner, and then either transferred to the *funduq* which corresponded to his nationality or retained in customs warehouses if his nation were unrepresented. Port taxes and duties (*droits au trésor*) were paid before transfer could be effected.

The customs service in the Muslim Maghrib was a highly stratified bureaucracy. In certain cities, notably Tunis and Bougie, the head of the service, sometimes called al-Caid and sometimes *musharrif* with no apparent distinction, was a member of the ruling nobility or not infrequently a prince of the blood. The director was not only protector but also intermediary between the European rulers and his own sovereign, to the extent of concluding treaties and being given full powers to negotiate commercial agreements. He also served as judge in legal disputes involving Christians and Muslims, and, in case of the death of a Christian belonging

9

to an unrepresented nation, the property and remains of the deceased passed into his care.

Custom sanctified by treaty governed all aspects of Christian-Muslim trade in the North African ports. Thus the boatmen who ferried goods off-loaded from vessels in the harbors into the dock areas received fixed salaries, as did the stevedores who transferred the merchandise from lighter to customs area. Nor were restrictions placed on sale of Christian merchandise once the customs duties had been paid; shipowners could dispose of their cargoes to Christian or Muslim purchasers alike.

The duties, although varying somewhat from state to state and port to port, were set in principle at between 10 per cent and 11.5 per cent ad valorem—usually 10 per cent, since European states trading with the Maghrib referred to it as the "tenth of obligation" in their commercial treaties. A 5 per cent duty, the "twentieth," was also levied. However, there were numerous exceptions. Jewelry, precious stones, and pearls and all other merchandise sold directly to local rulers or bought by the customs agents for the ruler's account were exempt from duty. There was no duty on ships sold within ports, irrespective of purchaser. Gold, unminted silver, rubies, pearls, and emeralds were subject only to a 5 per cent duty, but if re-exported unsold were exempt from the duty. Wheat, barley, and other cereals imported into the Maghrib were also exempted; the time when North Africa had been the granary of Rome was long past, and the region depended upon these shipments during periodic harvest failures.

Muslim rulers made frequent execptions to the normal 5 per cent export duty to encourage trade with the Christian world and at the same time stabilize their own positions vis-à-vis their rivals. Thus a Christian merchant could export duty-free merchandise equal in value to the amount he had imported to the Maghrib, whether he had paid import duties on it or not. Ownership of vessels based in a North African port which were rented to a European shipper entitled the exporter to duty-free exports up to the amount of the rental. However, numerous supplementary duties were levied by Maghrib customs authorities, sometimes fixed by custom, sometimes confirmed in treaties. Their suppression of these duties was a matter of great concern to Christian rulers in the rivalry for commercial advantage in the Mediterranean.

The treaty of 1323 between Abu Bakr, the Hafsid ruler of Tunis, and Jacques II of Aragon, which confirmed an earlier (1314) treaty between their predecessors, indicates some of these duties and fees. They included *inter alia*: fees for docking, anchorage, and harbor pilots (sometimes with anchorage cable and anchors provided by the port); the wages for boatmen and stevedores mentioned above; the *albara*, a special fee to the official designated by his sovereign's *berat* (official warrant) as over-all customs supervisor; a duty on weights and measures, such as one-half of olive oil per hundred jars off-loaded; the *rotl*, a duty applied as a measure of weight less than a kilogram to merchandise weighed and sold in sacks or bags; and the *tercumani* (Arabic *mursuruf*), fees paid for each use of translators or interpreters and usually set at 0.5 per cent per 100 valuation of merchandise.

The strict observance of these various regulations and the generally positive attitude of Maghribi rulers toward commerce with European states encouraged a steady growth in intra-Mediterranean trade. The products exchanged show clearly the evolving social pattern and mode of life of the urban Maghrib. From Europe came hunting birds, notably falcons and goshawks; raw and finished woods, imported for a variety of uses into timber-short North Africa (arrows, lances, loom spindles, serving utensils); and copper, second only to wood in importance as an import item. Europe also supplied precious metals used not only for currency but also in the fabrication of the jewelry with which the Maghribi bride arrayed herself before marriage and wore for the rest of her life as her dowry.

The fine silks, woolens, and cotton cloth of Europe found a ready market in the Algiers *suqs*; by the fourteenth century Burgundy lace, white curtain fabrics from Perpignan and Languedoc, the Italian fabrics called locally *Spiga* and *Sventoni*, English linen, velvet, satin, and taffeta were in common use in middle and upper-class Maghribi homes. Lacquers from northern Italy were also much in demand. Maghribi artisans purchased cinnabar, yellow arsenic, indigo, saffron, alum, and various dyes, while sulfur was much used in the whitening of the haiks of Algerine women. There was a brisk trade in French, Spanish, and Greek wines, for, although the greater share was destined for mercenary Christian soldiers in the pay of Maghribi rulers, there is no doubt that some was consumed by the Muslim citizenry, perhaps as a residual resentment of the puritanical Almohad attitude toward Islamic laxity of the previous century.

In turn Algiers and its neighbors exported a variety of commodities to Europe. There was some traffic in black slaves brought from sub-Saharan Africa to the North African ports. The Maghrib also exported to Europe Barbary horses, salted fish, leather hides and skins both dressed and raw, salt, wax, grain, vegetable dyes, coral, olive oil, dates, and a few other agricultural products. Barbary horses, famed for their endurance and trained for war on the high plateaus of North Africa, were much sought after by European knights and rulers. When the tide turned in favor of the Christians in Spain with the battle of Las Navas de Tolosa in 1212, Maghribi sovereigns ascribed the defeat to the new Spanish proficiency in cavalry warfare and for a time prohibited the export of horses to that land.

In the same way that the fabrics, woods, weapons, and metals of Europe shaped new standards of refinement for North Africa, North Africa's products generated a reverse flow of refining influences into Europe. Most of the leather used in Europe came from the Maghrib or from Muslim Spain; "Moroccan" and "Cordoban" were common adjectives which identified instantly a commodity highly prized from Edinburgh to Dubrovnik. The "bark of Bougie" was much in demand among Italian shoemakers in their work; it was known as *iscorza di Buggiea* and was mentioned in fourteenth-century tariff records of Pisa and Venice by that name. Bougie, Algiers, and Bona were the principal outlets for the wax and honey of Mauritania in the western Sahara. Mauritanian wax, called *cire de Bougie* by the French, ultimately became the French name for a particular type of candle.

Commerce between Algiers and European ports was sufficiently extensive to warrant regular calls by European merchant ships. For example, July was the month for Venetian and Florentine ships to call there, and from four to sometimes six vessels from each republic usually did so. But the deterioration in relations between the various Maghribi sovereigns which erupted into intermittent warfare in the fourteenth century not only obstructed this commerce but forced the Algerine merchants to think seriously about entrusting part of their hard-won local autonomy to some new protector.

An agreement was reached therefore, with the Arab Tha'liba tribe encamped around the city. The Tha'liba chiefs agreed to provide protection from raids or outright occupation by Hafsid, Marinid, or Ziyanid forces in return for tribute and trading concessions. In this fashion the Algerine citizens were able to attain a degree of security previously denied them. Administration of their city was in the hands of a merchant oligarchy comparable to those of Venice, Pisa, and other Christian city-states with whom the Algerines traded. From the early fifteenth century on Algiers was spared the internecine struggles and dynastic hatreds which sapped the vigor of its wealthier neighbors. Its autonomous status and relative inaccessibility behind its land walls and the protection of the Tha'liba made it a logical choice as the key forward base for the Islamic counter crusade against Latin Christianity led by the Ottomans following the *Reconquista* and the Spanish expansion into Africa of the early 1500's.

The capture of Constantinople by the Ottomans in 1453, the initial expulsion of Moriscos from Granada in 1492, the Spanish landings in North Africa, and the arrival of the Barbarossa brothers generated collectively a major change in the fortunes of Algiers. The ancient trading equilibrium of Muslim and Christian in the western Mediterranean was altered beyond redemption by these events. Such an equilibrium, based on mutual tolerance and a realistic assessment of the economic requirements of interdependent societies, could not long endure in the face of the militant expansionism of Spaniard and Turk and the replacement of local particularism by centralized authority.

A major element in this change was the development of piracy—in essence, the indiscriminate interference by outlaw ship captains with the peaceful conduct of trade by vessels of all nations, irrespective of flag—into an instrument of state policy. Certain European ports, notably those of Sicily, Sardinia, Corsica, and the Balearic Islands, were well known for the shelter and anchorage given to Christian freebooters who owed allegiance to no one. These corsairs preyed on Christian shipping more than on Muslim vessels; the records of Venice, Pisa, Marseilles, and other European merchant-republics are filled with complaints of corsair ravages.

Corsair activity out of the ports of the Maghrib was not as effective during this period as its European counterpart because of the inferior skill of North Africans in seamanship, navigation, and boarding operations; the absence of repair facilities; the much greater extent of European commerce; and the desire of Maghribi rulers to foster trade. Nonetheless, Christian privateering called for a slowly increasing response from the Muslims, until certain ports had acquired a parallel reputation. Mahdia, southeast of Tunis, had a well-organized corsair fleet as early as the thirteenth century, whose purpose was described by al-Bakri as being "to wage pirate warfare against the Christian countries." Bona also had its corsairs, while the largest corsair force, recruited from schismatic Ibadis (a Kharijite sect) in the Kabyle mountains, was based at Bougie.

The fall of Granada prompted a release of Spanish energies, so long paralyzed by the conflict over the peninsula, into overseas ventures. Africa, being close at hand, was the logical first choice for the restoration of Spanish fortunes. At the same time the emigration of the Moriscos created tension and provided a pretext for Spanish intervention. A short-lived Muslim insurrection in the mountains around Granada in 1501 and the discovery of an alleged Morisco conspiracy in Seville (its principals were believed to have entered into secret correspondence with the Ottoman sultan and various North African rulers toward a Muslim invasion) whetted fears in Spain of a Muslim counterattack.

In 1505 a Spanish armada went into action to forestall this possibility. Mers-el-Kebir, then Oran, then Bougie were captured in short order. Other Algerian ports, notably Tenès, Dellys, Cherchel, and Mostaganem, agreed to pay tribute and to abandon corsair activity in order to avoid a similar fate. In 1510 Algiers in its turn signed a treaty recognizing the sovereignty of Ferdinand the Catholic. The Algerines agreed to pay an annual tribute and sent a delegation to pay homage to the Spanish commander, Pedro Navarro, at Bougie. They also ceded to Spain one of the small islands protecting the harbor. Navarro built a fort on the island, which was renamed the Peñon. Spanish cannon dominated Algiers from a distance of three hundred yards, thereby enforcing the treaty and tribute. With the capture of Tripoli in 1511, Spain held an arc of territory controlled by garrisoned strongholds (presidios) across the entire top of the North African coast.

The citizens of Algiers resented not only this "dagger at their throats" but also the Spanish interference with their commerce. A decree of King Ferdinand's in 1511 imposed a 50 per cent surtax on their wool imports in order to pay the costs of the African expedition. The Tha'liba chiefs were no longer able to furnish protection against an island garrison which could be provisioned by sea. The Ottoman Turks were still far away and preoccupied with the consolidation of their continental territories and the clash with Safavid Persia. The Ottoman fleet had not yet experienced the growth which would make it equal to the combined navies of Christian Europe, and Islamic naval warfare awaited its true organizers and strategists.

In obedience to the Islamic tradition that obliges men to rush to the aid of whatever part of the *dar al-Islam* is threatened with physical danger or territorial occupation— the essential principle of jihad—volunteers from distant lands still belonging to Islam headed for the North African ports to combat the Spaniards. They came to offer their swords; even more valuable, successful corsair captains offered to enroll their vessels and entire crews in the service of whichever Maghribi ruler was willing to offer anchorage, pay, and facilities. The Hafsid rulers of Tunis, having greater resources, provided a kind of clearing house for the volunteers, much as the Byzantine emperors had done earlier for the Frankish crusaders on their way to Jerusalem. Since there was always the risk that hospitality might be rewarded with involvement in their internal affairs and a sudden change of masters, the Hafsids in particular encouraged their guests to move on if it became apparent that their ambitions lay elsewhere than in the advancement of the sacred war. By this policy Hafsid legitimacy was preserved, while the Algerian ports suffered, exchanging a precarious autonomy for incorporation into the most tightly controlled state to appear in the Maghrib.

The formation of this state resulted from the actions of two brothers known in Mediterranean folklore and European history as the Barbarossas. There were originally four brothers in the family, and, although there is much dispute concerning their origins, it is generally agreed that they came from the island of Medelli (Mytilene, the ancient Lesbos) off the Aegean coast of Turkey. The eldest of the brothers was Abu Yusuf Aruj ibn Yakub. Then followed Elias, Ishaq, and Khizr (Khidr) who received the epithet Kheireddin (Khayr al-Din), "the gift of God," probably because he was the youngest and hence was marked for a special future or the comfort of his parents' old age. Their father, Yakub, may have been a Muslim corsair, a Christian renegade, or, according to some authorities, a Janissary sergeant who had retired to the island and become a potter. Equal confusion surrounds the mother, who may have been the daughter of a Greek priest or an Andalusian woman captured by Yakub at sea.

Whatever the truth, the brothers pursued a marine vocation from an early age. Around 1501 Aruj and Elias were surprised at sea by a galley of the Christian Knights of St. John of Jerusalem, the order based at Rhodes which was then at war with the Ottomans. Elias was killed and Aruj was captured. For the next three years he labored at the oars of Christian galleys as the Knights pursued their conflict with the Turks—a conflict which would end in their expulsion from Rhodes and resettlement in Malta, where they became the principal rivals of the Algerine corsairs. Eventually Aruj was ransomed, probably by his father, and resumed his naval career.

By 1504 he and his two remaining brothers had reached the western Mediterranean, where Aruj carried his personal vendetta with Christianity into Spanish and Italian waters. The Hafsid sultan of Tunis offered him the governorship of Djerba, and from this base Aruj carried out a series of daring exploits which won him a great reputation. In addition to numerous Spanish prizes, he captured two large galleys belonging to the pope, and he was heavily involved in the transport of Moriscos to North African ports after the expulsion from Granada. Turkish and renegade recruits alike flocked to join his corsair squadron, which by 1510 numbered between ten and twelve vessels. His men called him Baba Aruj (Father Aruj) in token of their respect and dependence upon his leadership. It is probably this nickname, mispronounced by Europeans, rather than the auburn beards he and Kheireddin wore, that gave rise to the name "Barbarossa."

When the news of the death of King Ferdinand of Spain reached North Africa the three brothers were installed at the small port of Gigeri (Djidjelli) on the Kabyle coast east of Algiers. Although Aruj had been unsuccessful in two efforts to expel the Spaniards from Bougie, his naval reputation was such that the Algiers oligarchy decided to seek his aid in overcoming the Spanish garrison on the Peñon and ending the annual tribute. Their protector, the Tha'liba sheikh Salam al-Tawmi, who had been elected governor of the city and district, sent an emissary to Gigeri. Aruj, who by this time had won the support of the Banu Abbas tribe, marched overland with a force of three hundred Turks lent him by the Hafsid governor and a large contingent of Kabyles, and sent his brothers by sea with the corsair squadron. The combined force entered Algiers in 1516 and was received with acclamation by the citizens.

The agreement between the Algerines and their new protector specified that their municipal sovereignty would be respected, that they would not be subjected to new taxes or interference with their commerce, and that Aruj's assistance would be limited to the reconquest of the Peñon. But the Turkish cannon were ineffective against the fortress. With the harbor unusable, the corsairs were forced to haul up their boats on the exposed beach at Sidi Farraj, west of Algiers, to escape the Spanish guns. Meanwhile, Aruj, whose piety and seriousness of purpose had won him the full support of the population (he led prayers daily in the Almoravid mosque for the deliverance of the town from the infidels), began to arrogate to himself the functions of municipal authority. The public treasury was diverted to pay his Turks, while Kabyle chiefs and Turkish officers were placed in charge of customs, weights and measures, and market supervision, replacing the municipal officials who had held those responsibilities.

Salam al-Tawmi, seeing his governorship displaced, withdrew to the security of his tribe in the Mitidja. A conspiracy to oust the by now unwelcome visitors, whose behavior toward citizens had acquired the earmarks of a military occupation, was hatched by the Algerines with the cooperation of both the Tha'liba sheikh and the Spaniards. Aruj learned of it, lured Salam al-Tawmi back to Algiers with pledges of loyalty, and strangled him with his own turban in his bath as the unfortunate chief was preparing for his midday prayers. The unknown Arab chronicler of the

Ghazawat Aruj wa Khayr al-Din tells us that Aruj spread word that the sheikh had drowned in his bath; the Turks and Kabyles then took arms and conducted their chief, on horseback, to the Great Mosque, where they saluted him as king of Algiers. The Algerines accepted the situation without opposition. The son of their late protector, a boy of eleven, was spirited out of the town and escaped to Oran, where his presence served as the excuse for the subsequent Spanish expedition which cost Aruj his life.

The much greater exploits of his younger brother should not obscure the vital contribution of Aruj to the building of the Algerine state. A second uprising against his authority, this time by the municipal oligarchy itself, was suppressed ruthlessly; the doors of the mosque were locked during the Friday-noon prayer, and twenty-two principal citizens were bound and beheaded. Their heads were thrown into the streets and their bodies into the main sewer of Algiers. Thereafter, Aruj was master of Algiers, establishing the pattern whereby the Turks ruled and the rest of the population accepted their superiority without question. A more important contribution was the attachment of Algiers to the Ottoman Porte. Aruj signaled his triumph in a message to Sultan Selim I *Yawuz*, placed Algiers under Ottoman protection, and invited all ship captains not otherwise employed to join his standard in the sultan's wars in defense of Islam.

It is probable also that Aruj rather than Kheireddin established the basic principles of organization of Algiers. Authority was vested in the *ocak*, (literally, "hearth" in Turkish), the military garrison of Turks or Christian renegades recruited from elsewhere in the Ottoman possessions, under their own officers. Not only were native North Africans excluded from positions in the military government, but equally excluded were the *ḳul oğlarī*, sons of members of the *ocaḳ* by native women. Aruj was undoubtedly guided by his observation of the organization of the Knights of Rhodes, an equally exclusive military governmental order. To provide a religious sanction to this structure and thus make it palatable to his new subjects, Aruj applied the advice of the famous marabout, Sidi abd al-Rahman al-Talibi, the patron saint of Algiers, who had once said, "Leave the sea to the natives, never allow your sons to share in the government, and power will never escape from your hands."

It was certain that Aruj, as an ambitious soldier of fortune, would not remain long in Algiers, but would use the town as a base for expansion. Profiting by the rivalries of other Maghribi rulers and the divisive threat of Spain, he extended his personal authority as far west as Tlemcen. The Zirid triangle of Algiers-Miliana-Midiyah submitted to him, as did the Shalif Valley, part of the Djebel Dahra, the Ouarsenis range, the Mitidja, Cherchel (previously seized by a Turkish corsair named Car-Hassan) and the coast to the very gates of Oran. It was an extraordinary success, but it was ephemeral, endangering Spain's communications with her new African possessions and threatening an end to the authority of numerous petty rulers. A Hispano-Arab coalition formed against him, and in 1518 he was surrounded in Tlemcen and his brother Ishaq was captured and murdered by Arab tribesmen.

After a six months' siege, the city itself surrendered. Aruj managed to escape, but he was trapped and killed along with his Turkish bodyguards near the Oued Melh (Rio Salado, "River of Salt"). The Spanish officer who cut him down, one

Garcia de Tineo, was granted the right to incorporate the image of the corsair's head into his coat of arms. Aruj's head and jacket were sent to the governor of Oran, who subsequently gave the jacket to the Monastery of St. Jerome in Córdoba, where it adorned the wall of a chapel, long identified as *la capilla de Barbarossa*.

Under most circumstances the sudden death of the bold corsair would have created few ripples in the ever-churning seas of North African political history. Still less likely was it that Algiers would rise to dominate its neighbors and the entire western Mediterranean, or for that matter that it would remain for so long in Turkish hands. The dispossessed sultan of Tlemcen, restored to his throne with the help of his Spanish allies, was ready to march on Algiers. Meanwhile, the Spanish prepared a naval expedition under the command of Admiral Hugo de Moncada, viceroy of Sicily, to drive the Turks from the western Maghrib. The fleet dropped anchor off Algiers on August 17, 1518. Some fifteen hundred men from the landing force of seven thousand soldiers went ashore under the command of General Marino de Ribera, the hero of Oran, to fortify the hill which later became the *Fort de l'Empéreur*. There the Spaniards waited for the arrival of auxiliaries promised by the sultan of Tlemcen. It was a fatal mistake. Eight days later, on St. Bartholomew's Day, a tremendous storm wrecked most of their ships, and four thousand men were drowned. From then on "Well-guarded Algiers" (*Cezayir muhafazali*) seemed to enjoy the special protection and favor of Allah.

Before this stroke of good fortune, Kheireddin, who had remained in Algiers while Aruj marched on Tlemcen, was preparing to abandon the town and resume his corsair career.

Several of his subordinates convinced him to stay and struggle against adversity as befitted a true believer. The ever-fickle Algerines recognized him as his brother's successor and lord of Algiers. Kheireddin then sent an envoy to Ottoman Sultan Selim, pointing out the advantages of Algiers as a Muslim forward base for the struggle against the infidel and asking for assistance. Selim responded by dispatching two thousand Turkish Janissaries, and issued a firman to the effect that volunteers for the African campaign would be provided with free passage to Algiers and the assurance of enrollment at regular wages in the *ocak*. A later firman issued after the defeat of Moncada defined Algiers as an *eyalet* (border province) of the Ottoman Empire; the Venetian *bailli* resident at Constantinople was persuaded by the Ottoman grand vizier to issue a *laissez-passer* for use by Algerine vessels as units in the Ottoman fleet, and Kheireddin was authorized to coin money for circulation in the new territory. The return of the first Algerine mission to the Porte set a pattern for the sanctioning of government of the *ocak*. Kheireddin received from the sultan's emissary in formal ceremony the firman of appointment, which he read aloud before the citizens and the assembled militia of Algiers. The firman stated that the Padishah-i-Islam accepted the homage of the citizens, that he permitted them to issue money with his seal and use his name in the khotba and prayers, and that Kheireddin was thereby confirmed as lieutenant to the Padishah with the title of beylerbey of Algiers, commander of the *ocak*, and regent, acting in the name of the Padishah. In this fashion the Regency of Algiers came into existence.

From then on the Algerine state occupied a central and pivotal position in North Africa. In 1530 the Peñon of

Algiers was captured from the Spaniards after a sixteen-day bombardment. Using prisoner labor along with local carpenters and Morisco stonemasons, Kheireddin completed in two years a stone breakwater which linked the island to the mainland. His ships were now able to anchor inside an artificial harbor which protected them from the prevailing northerly and northwesterly winds, although the occasional nor'east squall remained a hazard, as Charles V of Spain would learn to his regret in 1541.

Kheireddin's corsair captains, notably Aydin Reis and Salah Reis, scored several brilliant victories over their Christian adversaries, one of the most successful being the capture of eight heavily armed Spanish galleys commanded by Admiral Rodrigues de Portundo off Mallorca, the favorite hunting ground of the corsairs. On land, Kheireddin extended the limits of the eyalet to roughly the present territory of Algeria, exclusive of the Sahara, although in the case of the Kabyles of the interior, agreement was reached to require of them no more than an oath of allegiance to the Ottoman sultan through his Algerine deputy. In 1534 the founder of the state of Algiers left the city which had gained him his reputation, never to return. He had already received from Sultan Süleyman I the caftan of honor and the title of Pasha of Three Horsetails. Now he was called to Constantinople to assume command of the Ottoman fleet as *kapudan derya*, "grand admiral." He left in Algiers his young son Hassan ibn Kheireddin under the joint guardianship of Pasha Çelebi Ramadan and Hassan Ağa, the commander of the *ocak*, the latter entrusted with supreme authority.

The new state sustained its most serious challenge seven years later. Before Hassan Ağa could fully organize its defenses, the fleet of Charles V, victorious at Tunis, anchored east of the new harbor while twenty-five thousand soldiers slowly disembarked along the estuary of the Oued el-Harraç. But ill luck dogged every stage of the expedition; the prophecy of "the sorceress of Algiers," cited by Marmol, which had predicted the destruction of Moncada's expedition, was repeated for the Holy Roman emperor's forces. A cold rain began to fall, followed by thick fog which isolated the infantrymen from their naval support. Then a violent northeast squall swept across the bay and destroyed the armada. Those Spaniards and their Maltese and other allies not drowned were hounded to death by the Turks and coastal Arabs. It seemed to many European leaders that Algiers was not only well guarded but totally secure under the protection of a mightier God than theirs.

II

THE WELL-GUARDED CITY

Hassan Ağa's successful repulse of the powerful Spanish expedition not only earned him near-marabout status among the faithful, but also encouraged the Ottoman sultan to continue the subsidy and investiture which together confirmed the Regency as part of his dominions. The *ocak* leader and his successor, al-Haci Bashir, were confirmed as pashas of the state until 1546, when Hassan ibn Kheireddin attained his majority. At that time authority was divided, with the grand admiral's son designated as beylerbey, the effective civilian head of the state, as distinct from the military commander of the *ocak*. However, communications from the Porte to Algiers were seldom if ever addressed to a single head of state, but rather to "Beylerbeyisi," along with other senior officials and the highest ranking dignitaries of the ulema. Not until the advent of the deys and the establishment of active diplomatic relations with Europe in the eighteenth century was there any serious effort to identify the Algerine state with a single leader, and, as will be seen in subsequent chapters, the deys usually disclaimed any pretensions to absolute sovereignty, preferring to describe themselves as the instruments of Allah.

The image of Algiers as an invincible bastion of Islam under the protection of both supernatural and visible powers, which so confounded Europe, was enhanced by the physical appearance of the city. The approach by land was, and remains, unimpressive; the city materializes abruptly below its crested barrier of hills with its masses of squat buildings squeezed between these hills and the broad bay beyond. But the maritime approach was calculated to inspire respect, even awe, for its aloof majesty. The enclosure of the harbor by Kheireddin created an effective naval base and laid the basis for appropriate urban institutions and structures. Construction proceeded uphill from the harbor, with Morisco artisans and workmen, along with Christian prisoners, laboring under Turkish overseers to set in place an urban design familiar to them from Ottoman port cities.

The successful development of this design made Algiers the most Turkish of all North African cities (a sort of Constantinople in miniature) in its layout, its harbor-front buildings, and its one long main street, while the grave silent men smoking their water pipes and the aroma of Turkish coffee recalled the origins of many of its citizens. Yet it was the military construction of the city, more than any other element, which reaffirmed for Europeans that legend of Algerine invincibility created by the Turks that for three centuries cast a long shadow across the Mediterranean. Nicholas Nicolay, who halted there en route to Constantinople on a mission from the French court to the Porte, saw Algiers as "situated upon the Mediterranean upon the hanging of a mountain environed with strong Walls, Ramparts, Bulwarks, in form almost three-square. . . ." William Davies, the barber-surgeon of a captured British ship, wrote in 1597 of his place of captivity, "Algiers is a marvelous strong city and governed by the Turk, lying upon the side of an upright hill, strongly fortified with forts, castles and platforms with great store of ordnance." A common descriptive term for the city was to liken it to a bent bow, perhaps an appropriate symbol for an Ottoman forward base pointed toward Christian lands.

Seen at close range, the aura of majestic power and of unfathomable mystery which cloaked the well-guarded city at a distance fell away to reveal a well-planned urban center which took full advantage of its peculiar terrain. Ottoman Algiers was built in the form of a triangle. Its apex was the Kasba, from whence it sloped steeply down to the sea. Behind the harbor defenses and fortifications lay the so-called "lower city," where most of Algiers' commercial activity and day-to-day living took place. This sector was crossed by a single through street, Grand Market Street (*Büyük Çarsi*), reminiscent of the main street in Constantinople with its numerous zigzags intersected by alleys and crowded with shops, cafés, and market stalls. There were two gates, barred by heavy iron doors, at each end—*Bab el-Oued* (frequently used by Europeans to describe the entire street because it had a specific name) on the northwest corner and *Bab ez-Zoun* on the southeast corner. A third gate, Bab Cedid (New Gate), provided access from the Kasba to the lower city. From the ground level the masses of white buildings rose skyward, capped by flat roofs overhung with terraces, which gave shade and flowers to Algerine citizens as they enjoyed their view across the sparkling bay toward the distant Mediterranean.

The well-guarded city fully deserved its epithet in terms of the fortifications built by the Turks. They developed its defenses with great care and a high degree of engineering skill, and maintained them with equal vigor, so that as a military establishment Algiers outshone other Ottoman cities, including the imperial capital itself. By the early 1600's a moated wall twelve feet in depth and ranging in elevation from forty feet along the harbor to thirty feet on the inland side ringed the entire city. The "Round Castle" built by the Spaniards while they were masters of the Peñon was refurbished with three tiers of guns, mostly thirty-six-pounders. The Kasba was enclosed with a separate octagonal wall fitted with cannon embrasures that dominated the outer bay; several other castles and forts supplied additional firepower for the defense of Algiers. The total firepower was considerable; Angelo Emo, admiral of the Venetian fleet, who visited the city in 1767 on a mission to renew the peace treaty of 1763 between Venice and the Regency, counted 140 very large cannon along the harbor and 300 smaller guns emplaced elsewhere.

The citizens who dwelt behind this impressive array of fortifications were a multiethnic lot who nevertheless coexisted harmoniously under Turkish military rule. Although the keeping of accurate demographic statistics had to await the arrival of the French, we can estimate the total population from the accounts of various observers. Again, the impression projected by Algiers abroad was deceptive, as the total seems to have fluctuated between one hundred and one hundred and thirty thousand over the three hundred years of Regency existence. A difficulty with enumeration was the practice of listing households rather than individuals; thus an observer such as Haedo, who as a Christian was not permitted inside Muslim homes, but who managed to count houses during his peregrinations about the city, provides no yardstick as to family size. Yet these households themselves remained surprisingly constant—12,200 in 1580, 13,000 in 1610, and 20,000 in 1816. Pananti, whose status as a freed captive enabled him to move about the city easily and mingle with the various groups, thought that there were approximately one hundred and twenty thousand citizens in Algiers. In the mid-seventeenth century, apart from the government and the *ocak*, there were in Algiers 2,500 households of *baldis* (freeborn Algerine Muslims); 700 Kabyle households; 200 Morisco households; 1,600 families of *kul oğlari* (sons of Janissary Turks by Maghribi women); plus 16,000 renegade Christian individuals and approximately 12,000 Jews.

This city, "very like an egg in its fullness of houses and people," as one visitor saw it, took full advantage of its natural setting and the presence of a cosmopolitan citizenry to provide its residents with excellent urban amenities and a style of life consciously designed with them in mind. Nicolay, on disembarking, wrote:

Beyond the Pallace Royal are very fair houses belonging to particular men, with a great number of Bathes and Cookes houses. The places and streetes are so well ordained that everyone is in his Occupation apart—there are about three thousand hearthsteeds. At the bottom of the Citie is by great Artifice and subtill Architecture builded their principall and head Mosque. . . . this Citie is very Merchant-like, for that she is situated upon the Sea and for this cause marvellously peopled for her bigness.

Gramaye observed of seventeenth-century Algiers, "The King's Palace and great men's houses have courts spacious and many byroomes. . . . there are seven fair mosques, five Colleges of Janissaries where 600 live together in a house, one Hospital built by Hassan Pasha, four fair baths" (probably those referred to by Haedo as serving also as quarters for slaves and Christian captives).

By the eighteenth century development had proceeded to the point of endowing Algiers with facilities equal to those of any other Mediteranean city. The water supply, drawn traditionally from five cisterns outside the walls, had been supplemented by aqueducts built under the direction of a Morisco engineer from Granada, one of many whose technical skills were put to use by the Turks. Algerine households were well furnished with water for drinking and washing as a result, beyond that available from their own small wells. The city benefited from the endowment of public baths (hammams) and fountains. A marble fountain with a waterfall spout splashed day and night before the palace of the beylerbeys in Haedo's time, and throughout the city several thousand smaller fountains rendered agreeable the cafés and shops in the various public squares of Algiers. Large hammams had been built by Hassan Pasha and Muhammad ibn-Sala Reis, the grand captain of the Algerine navy, of finest marble, equipped with hot and cold water, and equal of the finest hammams in Constantinople. The *banyolar* (barracks) assigned to Christian prisoners, far from being the dank holes which gave rise to European legends of slave mistreatment, were comparable in amenities to the quarters of the *ocak*. Thus the Grand Banyo, wherein captives belonging to the state itself were housed, was a large building, seventy by forty feet, divided into small rooms, with a cistern in the middle. Below, at ground level, was an oratory where mass was said regularly for Catholic prisoners.

As the Algerine state increased in wealth, members of its elite, particularly the commanders (*reisi*) of the corsair establishment, began to adopt a suburban mode of living, building country villas outside the city. However, this exodus never seriously affected the urban dominance of Algiers, and there was never any question of a division of responsibilities with other cities within its territory, such as Oran or Constantine, or of the centripetal tendencies which fragmented other North African states, notably Morocco, or delayed the progress of national identity in Europe. Algiers was where the action was and its citizens were well aware of their elitist status in the Islamic world. The walls that encircled their city gradually crumbled during the three centuries of peace within the Regency's borders, but the tradition of a well-guarded urban center persisted, just as the constant maritime activity drew the citizens harborwards to such a degree that when Exmouth's flagship anchored along the mole in 1816 the entire population gathered to watch its arrival, only dispersing rapidly uphill when the English opened fire.

Until Dey Ali moved his household into the Kasba for

safety in the nineteenth century, the residence of the beylerbeys (and their successors) was in the center of the lower city facing, opposite its main entrance, a broad plaza about two hundred and forty feet in circumference. The entrance was flanked by two arcaded galleries, supported by marble pillars, which extended the full width of the building. At the rear were two large halls where the Divan met three times weekly—Sunday, Monday, and Wednesday—to deal with affairs of state. Although the absence of European-style furniture created the impression of a certain bareness in this most elegant of Algerine buildings, it had a vast collection of mirrors, clocks, and weapons of every description, while the deep-pile carpets on the floors and walls imparted an Oriental sumptuousness to the western headquarters of Ottoman Islam.

The combination of limited terrain for construction purposes and the requirements of a marine vocation assured the growth of Algiers along compact, predictable lines. Consequently, there were few of the sharp divisions into quarters characteristic of other Islamic cities such as Fez, Cairo, or Damascus. In fact, Algiers under the Turks may well have been the most homogeneous of cities, designed for its citizens and built in response to their needs. The Büyük Çarsï was the widest street, thirty-six feet wide according to one estimate, yet even this street was barely wide enough to accommodate the jostling throng that used it. Elsewhere, Algiers' streets were a veritable rabbit warren. They had no names, and the lack of organized handicraft guilds meant that such familiar appellations as "street of the dyers" or "spice market" could not be used to identify them; residences and vocations were intermingled on every street. Other than the "marine quarter" near the harbor where most of the corsairs lived, every section of Algiers was polyglot in its background and indistinguishable from its neighbors, a fact emphasized by the private, family-oriented nature of Muslim society. The development of slums and lower-class workmen's neighborhoods did not take place until the arrival and colonization of the French.

An aspect of Algiers' layout which fascinated Europeans was the narrowness of the streets, "so joined to one another that it seems like a thick pine," Haedo tells us, and so narrow that a man on horseback could barely pass through them, while two people could not walk abreast. Paving material was rough cobbles, aranged to slope inward from the walls of the houses (there were no sidewalks) toward a central drain. One can still see many streets in the Kasba of Algiers today with this type of construction. Not only were the streets narrow, but the houses and buildings along them also sloped inward as they rose from ground level, with the roofs practically joined at the top so as to shut out the sunlight. However, the disadvantages of narrow passage and poor visibility had its compensating features. During the hot, damp summer the streets conserved the early morning coolness throughout the day, and there was much less humidity than at higher levels or in the miasmic, malarial inland plains of Algeria. Damage from earthquakes—Algiers suffered heavily from them in 1717 and on several other occasions—was lessened by the tapering construction. Intraurban movement was further facilitated by the terraces atop each house, so that Algerine ladies could pass easily from house to house and by means of ladders cross the entire city without being seen publicly or having to descend to the street.

Algerine houses were built on a standard ground plan, consisting of a square tower with suites of rooms around the four sides. The houses varied only in size and in the value of construction materials and interior decorations. The United States Consulate in the 1800's was constructed as follows, so Consul William Shaler tells us:

It is a square of sixty-four feet, with a depth, or elevation, of forty-two feet, one third of which is occupied by the basement story consisting of a range of magazines, cisterns, stables and the solid arches necessary to support the super-structure. It has two habitable stories, surounding the open court paved with marble, thirty feet square, around which is a covered gallery six feet wide, supported by twelve very elegant columns of Italian marble, which serve as abutments to twelve elliptical arches and thus form around the court a double colonnade of great elegance and beauty. The roof is flat, and terraced, with a parapet of about four and a half feet high, and on the side fronting the sea there is a third covered gallery. . . . the apartments are narrow and long beyond all proportion, well enough calculated for this climate.

The sides of the houses that faced the sea had windows, but generally speaking there were no external windows, on the theory that these would enable men to observe their neighbors' wives. The flat roofs served many purposes, such as for the collection of rainwater, for doing laundry, and for the gossip rites of the women.

The most common building material used in Algiers was tabby, a kind of cement made of wood ashes, lime, and sand in three-to-two-to-one proportions mixed with oil and beaten with shovels or wooden mallets for three consecutive days, after which it became as hard as marble, although a great deal easier to work with. A mixture of pitch and lime was used to join the pipes which brought water into the city along the aqueducts and distributed it into cisterns for public buildings and private houses. In this respect the Algerines showed themselves equal as builders to the Romans; their cisterns, arches, terraces, and building façades appeared to visitors to be as firm and compact as if they had just been built, long after the fact.

Fear of earthquakes and a certain wish for exterior uniformity set limits on the height and decoration of buildings in Algiers. Almost all the houses were two or three stories, the mosques and the palace having three. Entry was by a single door. The doors were an exception to the general plainness; they were of solid wood heavily studded with iron, and often boasted handsome wrought iron or brass handles and knockers. These knockers were often in the design of the *khamsa*, the five-fingered hand common in Mediterranean symbolism and identified by Muslims with the hand of the Prophet Muhammad's daughter Fatima. Leading Algerine citizens who had been to Constantinople brought back with them Turkish designs and motifs which they applied to public and private decoration, a common motif being the artichoke. The door of a house, like the gates in the city wall, marked the line dividing friend from foe, intimate from stranger. The privacy of Algerine families assured in this fashion was very different from the exuberant family life of European Mediterranean cities and was much commented on by European visitors.

The public gravity of Turkish Algiers found appropriate expression in its mosques. The seven fair ones of Gramaye's time numbered ten large and fifty small mosques by the time of the French conquest. Their design was plain and simple, copied from those of Turkey and the Levant. The Grand Mosque, built in 1790 facing the harbor, was a three-story structure measuring 180 by 120 feet, and was supported on three sides by columns of Geonese marble. It was the most beautiful public structure in Algiers after the dey's palace. The "New Mosque" (*Yeni Cami*), fronting on what is now Place Abdul Kader, was said to have been designed by a Christian prisoner in the form of a Greek cross, the design having somehow escaped the notice of the Turkish authorities.

One distinction commented on by travelers to Algiers who were familiar with the eastern portions of the Ottoman Empire was that of the minaret design. Algerine minarets were quadrangular in shape and approximately the size of European clocktowers, quite unlike the round or polygonal minarets of the eastern Islamic lands, and lacking their fluting or delicate stone tracery.

Another link with the mother country was in Algerine funeral structures. The mausoleums of the deys—the two-story polygonal kubbas topped by a cupola—were modeled on those of the Ottoman sultans at Bursa, while the Turkoman *yurt* inspired the half-ovoid tombs of lesser persons.

Such was the general appearance of Turkish Algiers, a city with an urban design appropriate to its setting, its maritime vocation, and the mixed character of its population. The narrow streets facilitated the movement and interchange of these diverse peoples—Kabyles; Arabs; men from Biskra who served as water carriers for thirsty pedestrians; Moriscos, busy at their craftwork; Jews in their distinctive garb; prisoners being marched to work in the quarries and the arsenal by Ottoman overseers; and striding through their midst the lordly Janissary, sovereign over all though he might be merely a private soldier just recruited for the *ocak*. Yet Algiers' rulers were less feared than respected by its citizens. They provided entertainment, prestige, and wealth for the city, and there was no reason to challenge their rule. When an Algerine ship anchored along the mole, flying its green ensign spangled with silver stars around a crescent moon, crowds flocked to the harbor to watch it unload its captured cargo and display its prisoners. It was a time for buying and selling, for speculation, and for the high fever of excitement. Even the bad days, those on which the *ocak* quarreled or the Divan was split into factions over the succession question, passed quickly, as did the bombardments by European squadons. And life flowed on for residents of a city most favored of all Islamic cities by the blessing of Allah, guarded by an effective patron saint whose guarantee was that of invincibility, and backed by the resources of the mighty Ottoman Empire.

III

PATTERNS OF GOVERNMENT

In the area of administrative organization the Turks set a definite seal upon Algiers. Theirs was a city-state in the strictest sense of the term, endowed with a ruling institution which was clearly defined and kept separate from the mass of the people. Yet the same combination of accommodation to existing political conditions and judicious use of force which had marked the Ottoman expansion elsewhere was utilized to full effect to give Algiers a territorial identity. Turkish sovereignty extended from the Trara Mountains in the western *beylik* (province) of Oran eastward to the mouth of a small river near El Kala (La Calle), and southward into the Chott Djerid, identical with the present Tunisian-Algerian border. On the west, Algerine territorial limits extended from the port of Hunein (no longer functioning) southward through the Trara into the Sahara, then, as now, including Tlemcen but not the Moroccan cities of Oujda and Figuig. The installation of Ottoman officials in Tunis and Tripoli and the recognition by the Ottoman sultan of Saadian, later Alawite, sovereignty over Morocco laid the basis for the modern fourfold division of North Africa. Three of the four independent states were the product of European political structures grafted onto a Turkish base.

The cornerstone of Ottoman administration in Algiers was the *ocak*, the Janissary garrison recruited from elsewhere in the empire, assigned to the territory on a more-or-less permanent basis, and set apart by vocation and status from the rest of the Algerine population. The elitist nature of the parent Janissary order was applied with peculiar force in Algiers. Each recruit obtained for the *ocak*, regardless of his economic circumstances or social background, was made aware from his arrival in the corsair city that he belonged to a ruling group which had a controlling interest in Algerine government. As such, he had every inducement to defend the Regency and maintain its governing structure. In a political sense the state was his personal property. In an economic sense, the more it prospered the more he profited.

The internal factionalism and the changes in ruling nomenclature which evolved over the centuries of Turkish rule neither changed this basic relationship nor disturbed the Regency's inner harmony; these changes merely added layers to the bureaucratic organization of Algiers. In some respects the *ocak* may be compared with the Order of the Knights of St. John of Jerusalem during their sojourn on Malta. Both were *orders* in the sense of being separate ruling institutions implanted in alien soil and of having come into existence through response to appeals for a religious crusade. The Algiers *ocak*, however, governed a much larger territory, was nearly always on the offensive, and dominated western Mediterranean affairs well beyond the decline of its chief naval adversary.

The original pact between Baba Aruj and the notables of Algiers specifying that they would not be taxed for special obligations (such as wartime levies) in return for Ottoman protection was kept by his successors, so that, although the indigenous Algerines might be and indeed often were victimized by members of the *ocak*, collectively little was required of them beyond obedience, loyalty to the state, and respect for public order. Inasmuch as the majority of both rulers and ruled was Muslim, a commonality of interest prevailed in any case.

A further distinction between the *ocak* and its subjects was defined in terms of law. All Muslim citizens of the Regency were subject to Islamic Sharia (canonical law) as interpreted by Hanafi prescript. In civil matters they were also required to obey the *kanuni* (regulations) issued periodically by the Ottoman sultans and enforced by the *ocak*. But the responsibility for discipline and the behavior of the *ocak* was vested exclusively in its *aġa* (agha). Only the agha could order punishments imposed on individual Janissaries, and these could be issued only for violations of its internal regulations. Otherwise the order was inviolate, immune from civil suit or arrest by non-Turkish Algerines.

The ruling spirit of the *ocak* was absolute democracy. In Algiers the emphasis on ability and performance rather than

birth or family connections which marked the early Ottomans was preserved throughout the period of the Regency.
Recruitment for Janissaries was carried out largely among
the common people of Anatolia and the Mediterranean port
cities. Their pay was the same for all, and promotion in the
ranks was entirely by seniority. The recruitment was carried
out by corsair vessels, which paid annual calls at the principal
Ottoman harbors of the eastern Mediterranean. The thousand or so Anatolian recruits thus acquired were hustled
aboard ship before they could change their minds—although
the alluring prospects presented to them by Algerine Turkish
officers invariably seemed preferable to a miserable life in
their depressed Anatolian villages or decaying urban water-
fronts. The raw recruit upon arrival in Algiers was greeted
by his new comrades with derisive shouts such as, "Here
comes another stupid bull from Anatolia!" He was then
assigned to a particular barracks, and the number of his room
was tattooed on the back of his left hand. This made him a
yoldaş, the lowest rank of the *ocak*. After three years the *Yeni*
(new) *yoldaş* was saluted by his comrades as *Eski* (old)
yoldaş, and in another three years he became *Baş yoldaş*, or
squad leader of a *seffara* (tent) of sixteen to twenty men,
the basic Janissary troop unit.

Thereafter each promotion in rank in the *ocak* came in
steady, predictable sequence by seniority, until the private
soldier reached the rank of *vekilhardji* (sergeant major).
After this there were five officer ranks: *odabaşı* (lieutenant),
bolukbaşı (captain), *aghabaşi* (commander), *kahya* (colonel), and *ağa* or Agha (general). Each agha held his position for two months, after which he became a member of the
Divan and was succeeded by the senior *kahya*. At the end of

43

these successive terms of service the *yoldaş*, assuming he had not been killed, reassigned, or transferred to Constantinople or some other part of the empire, now became *mansoulagha* and was pensioned off, although he retained the right to keep his membership in the Divan.

The term of service in each rank was three years, spent in alternate one-year units of duty in *nouba* (garrison) and *mahalla* (field expeditions). The *mahallas* were important in showing the flag in remote and border areas and in the collection of tribute and taxes from nominally autonomous Algerian tribes. In this fashion the Turks were able to govern a large territory at small expense with a determined, disciplined body of men.

Although the *ocak* was modeled on the parent Janissary organization of Constantinople, its distance from the Ottoman capital and the exclusivity of the Turks as a ruling class endowed the individual *yoldaş* with an extraordinary status in Algiers. Following a brief period of indoctrination by his *eski* comrades and the issuance of his uniform of turban, vest, baggy trousers, slippers, and two pistols, which he stuck in his broad silver-buckled belt, the Anatolian bull swaggered into the streets to be saluted by the indigenous Algerines as "*Effendi.*" His relatively modest pay—which will be dealt with subsequently—was more than compensated for by his extensive rights and privileges, apart from the democratic promotional procedures outlined above. He was exempt from all taxes and duties, and was at liberty when off duty to follow any gainful occupation, learn a trade, or (after 1568) to ship aboard a corsair vessel. The only restriction on his movements was that he be ready to defend the state against enemies when called upon. All Janissaries shared in the distribution of prizes brought back by the corsairs, whether or not they had participated in the actions. Unmarried members were housed free of charge in large, clean barracks, furnished with low divans, tables, pillows, and mats, housing twelve to twenty men per room. Those under age were restricted to the barracks except for Thursdays, when they were permitted to go out under the supervision of a guardian. As soon as they could display a respectable growth of beard, this restriction was lifted!

The pay of the *ocak* was both in cash and kind. Each man received four loaves (two pounds) of bread a day, plus cooking oil and meat, for which he paid one-third the prevailing market price. Additional clothing and weapons were also furnished at little cost. These weapons consisted of pistols, a scimitar—a curved dagger worn either in the belt or inside the vest—and a long musket (for field duty only) carried on the shoulder. Cash payments were made according to a fixed scale. The newest and youngest *yoldaş* received (in Pananti's time) four *sümün* (Four *sümün* were computed by Shaler as $1.00. Pananti tells us that the senior Janissaries in service received about two pounds ($9.60).) every two months, payable in silver, one *sümün* being equal to 101 *dirhem sağīr*, or *akças*, the small, roughly square coins of low silver content which Europeans called aspers, or aspres). His pay increased slowly, at the rate of 50 *dirhems sağīr* per year, with special increases on the occasion of a great victory or the appointment of a new dey, to a maximum of 160 *sümün*. Pay, however, was stabilized at the end of the thirteenth year of service, after which no further increases were granted.

Each member of the *ocak* received his pay in person, in gold or silver coins according to the sums due him. He was

45

required to be present and to answer when his name was called. If he were absent by reason of being on *mahalla* or for some other excuse, he had to wait until the next bimonthly payday and even then could receive a reprimand along with his aspers. The order of payment was by rank and seniority, the sole variation being that the dey, as first soldier of the republic, received his pay first and in a double portion. Since none of the officers of the state received a fixed salary, the cost of administration was minimal.

The pay of the *ocak*, although small, was the one expense met regularly by the Public Treasury. This is one instance of the influence of the soldiery on government affairs. Whether on *mahalla*, in garrison, or participating in the elections of deys, they were the principal instrument of state authority, and their small pay as noted was well compensated for by special privileges and status. The one group capable of opposing them on any given occasion was the corsair guild, and its influence on Algerine government should not be overlooked.

The corsair profession (*il corso*), an ancient if not always honorable activity, was followed at various times by peoples as diverse as the Vikings, Arabs from the Hadhramaut and the Omani coast, Elizabethan adventurers, the "sea-robbers over the brine" mentioned in *The Odyssey*, and the Javanese pirates who ranged the Sulu Sea. But the true hub of corsair activity was the Mediterranean, a region where nature, geography, and navigational requirements provided near-perfect conditions for extralegal adventurism. The topography of the Mediterranean coasts and islands either severely circumscribed agriculture or precluded its development altogether.

Mediterranean men had little choice except to turn to the sea for their livelihood, in the face of such discouraging economic prospects. Yet fishing, albeit an occupation which offered a fair return for minimum investment, could hardly compare with the alluring prospects of systematic interference with the legitimate commercial vessels which plied the Mediterranean. Hundreds of small harbors provided shelter for the corsair vessel fleeing from a larger or better-armed opponent and a secret place where it could lay to while refitting. The true corsair was a professional man, proud of his navigational skill, his daring, the tactics he used to bring in prizes. If he were brought to justice in maritime courts, he identified himself as *corsale* or *korsan*, never as fugitive or criminal; his occupation was as clearly identifiable as that of tanner, goldsmith, potter, or baker.

Establishment of the Turks in Algiers formalized corsair activities in the Mediterranean into an institution. A well-organized system of recruitment, organization, financing, and operations governed the *taife reisi* from its inception in Algiers. The Algerine system became in turn the model for the *taife* in Tunis, Tripoli, and the short-lived "Republic of the Bou-Regreg" established by the corsairs of Rabat- Salé in Morocco. Corsairs were recruited from three principal sources—Christian renegades, Muslims from elsewhere in the Ottoman Empire, and a minority from the non-Turkish population of the Regency. Most of the great captains came from the first-named source, although in many cases (including the Barbarossas themselves) the ethnic background was mixed. Very few Maghribis attained high rank in the corsair fleet. Reis Hamida, the captain who captured Pananti and commanded the fleet during the Napoleonic Wars, was the exception, being a Kabyle without a drop of Turkish blood in his veins.

Like any other naval establishment, the *taife* had ranks and a system of progress through the ranks to that of captain. Reis Hamida, whose father was a tailor, is known to have shipped aboard a corsair vessel as cabin boy and advanced through merit and service to common sailor, mate, officer, then reis, before acquiring the command of the fleet. The normal procedure was for corsair captains to be chosen by the owners of the ships used in their campaigns, but before a captain could receive an appointment he had to pass an examination given by the Divan of the Reisi, a governing council which consisted of all captains who held commands at the time. A second institutional factor for the *taife* was provided by residence. Captains, crews, and suppliers all lived in the western quarter of Algiers, along the harbor and docks area below the Kasba. Here they could protect themselves against sudden onslaughts by their rivals of the *ocak*, and if necessary move in a body to the palace to participate in major policy deliberations.

The *taife* depended for its financing both on private individuals and the public purse. Because of the potential profits to be made from corsair prizes, the underwriting of expeditions was an attractive proposition. Shareholding was organized in the same manner as that of a modern stock company, with the return to individuals dependent on their investment. This type of private ownership reached its peak in the seventeenth century, the "golden age" of the Regency corsairs; thereafter the Algerine government underwrote the majority of expeditions and owned most corsair vessels.

Investors in the corsair system came from all levels of society in Algiers, ensuring a steady enlargement of the middle class as corsair success increased. A typical ownership arrangement included merchants, government officials, Janissary officers, shopkeepers, artisans, and ordinary citizens who had pledged their small savings. Sometimes the owner was the reis himself, or the owner might seek financial aid for refitting or for the purchase of timbers, supplies, or naval stores. Shipbuilding and the refitting of captured enemy vessels were the chief sources of employment for the Algerine labor force. The shortage of skilled labor was filled by prisoners or by renegades, carpenters, cannon founders, and armorers being in greatest demand, so that they fetched the highest prices in the auction market.

The division of captured cargo was governed by strict rules. After the state's share—committed to the dey as the representative of Allah in Algiers—had been deducted, fixed charges were paid to the port authorities and customs brokers, and to the upkeep of the sanctuaries of the marabouts whose intercession had made possible the success of the expedition. The net value of the cargo was then divided equally among the ship's owners and the crew. A further division of these two portions was then made, for the owners on the basis of each individual investment, and for the crew according to a complicated formula. In the late eighteenth century, for example, a corsair captain was entitled to 40 parts, ordinary seamen to 3, captured Christian seamen to 3, cabin boys to 1, Janissaries aboard the corsair to $1\frac{1}{2}$, out of a total of several hundred parts. After the cargo had been divided in this fashion, it could be resold either at auction or more commonly to European commercial representatives resident in Algiers, through whom it might even reach the port of its original destination. The combination of sale of prisoners and resale of cargo was the principal source of wealth for individuals in Algiers.

Over-all authority in Algiers passed through four stages during the Regency's existence. The first stage was that of the beylerbeys, officials appointed by the Ottoman sultan directly and subject to replacement. In the second stage, rulers were pashas appointed for three-year terms. Subsequently, the growth in size and power of the *ocak* and the organization of the corsairs led to the assumption of power by the aghas of the *ocak* with the advice and consent of the Divan. The fourth stage was the establishment of the office of dey, filled after 1689 by an elected member of the *ocak*. The authority of the deys was often severely restricted by the *ocak* through its own governing body, the Divan, or council of state. At one stage of the Regency there were two governing bodies, the Grand Divan and the Little Divan. The former was composed of the twenty-four senior officers of the *ocak*, the latter of some seven hundred officers and Janissary servants, as always ranked by age and seniority. However, only the members of the Grand Divan were called together regularly for deliberations. In the eighteenth century they met four times a week, on Monday, Wednesday, Thursday, and Saturday, at the M'lakma, the palace of the pashas, within the complex of buildings known as the Dar al-Sultan. Sometimes the senior members of the ulema were permitted to share in the deliberations, and the number of members varied. Dr. Shaw counted thirty "pashas" in attendance at its sessions. Members of the Divan wore a strip of gold lace pinned to the front of their turbans to identify their status.

Sessions of the Divan were colorful and impressive. On special occasions all the pomp and pageantry of the Ottoman court itself was recreated in the corsair capital. Here is the description by the Dutch Redemptorist priest Père Dan of the investiture of Abd al-Hassan Ali in 1634 upon his arrival from Constantinople as the new triennial pasha:

The city sent out two well-equipped galleys to do him honor. The officer corps of the Divan assembled in the number of five hundred to receive him at the port, where as he disembarked from his galley he was received with a salute of some fifteen hundred guns from the city forts and the corsair ships some forty of which came out under sail. There then marched the Agha of the Janissaries accompanied by two drummers (Çavuş), followed by the Principal Secretary with the 24 Ayabashis who are the chief Counselors of State. There followed two by two the Bulukbashis with their huge plumed turbans, then the ranks of the Odabashis; there marched after them six Turkish oboists with Moors among them some playing flutes and other cymbals, the whole ensemble a very strange noise which aroused in us more fear than pleasure. Last came the new Pasha, enveloped as a mark of peace in a vast white robe. He rode a fine Barbary steed richly harnassed with a silver bridle studded with gems, spurs and stirrups, reins of silk all laden with turquoises and an embroidered saddle-cloth elaborately worked. In this order the procession entered the city and the Pasha was taken to the residence designated for him.

Sessions of the Divan were characterized by a completely egalitarian procedure. The agha, as presiding officer, proposed the subject of deliberation, which was repeated in a loud voice by the *ḳahyas*, and then echoed by the four senior *aghabaṣis*, in unison. From there it was passed along from member to member, seated in two rows back to back, one row facing east, the other west, until the entire membership had spoken. The vote was taken in the same manner. Unanimity of balloting and discussion enabled the council to dispose of a great deal of business in rapid order, all resolutions being noted by the second-ranking agha, who served as secretary. Proceedings invariably were finished in less than three hours. On the occasions of the election of a new dey or significant issues such as a peace treaty, the entire *ocaḳ* was required to be present. The soldiers stacked their weapons outside the mirrored meeting hall and sat cross-legged with their arms folded during deliberations.

In its bureaucratic organization, the Algerine state also took its cue from its Ottoman parent. Most of the administrative officers were duplicates of those found in the Ottoman state government. The peak of bureaucratization came in the eighteenth century. During this period there were four officials who composed collectively a "Council of Secretaries of State." They were the *veḳilhardji*, (or minister of marine), who was responsible for the military establishment and the maintenance of the arsenal and shipyard; the *hazinedar* (*ḳhaznadji*), or grand treasurer, responsible for the economy, finances, and production; the *hoca el-ḳeil*, or administrator of customs; and the agha of the Algiers garrison. They supervised a corps of minor officials who may be grouped for the sake of convenience into several categories—military, supervisory and legal security, and economic. Responsible to the *hazinedar*, for example, were the *beit el-medji* (sequestrator of unclaimed property and supervisor of cemeteries), the *saidjis* (cashiers), and the *emin-essekiya* (controller of the currency).

A large number of officials in all three categories were called *hocas* (literally "teacher"), in part because they were literate, but also because of their alleged or real intellectual attainments. The ranking official in this group was the *baş-hoca* (*baş* means "head"). Another *hoca* served as the pasha's private secretary, another as the supervisor of granaries (*makhzan*). Other learned gentlemen who duplicated Ottoman bureaucratic functions included: the director of the monopoly on salt (*hoca el-milh*), on hides (*cild*), the receiver of customs (*gumruk*), the supervisors of weights and measures (*uzan*), and the *hoca* charged with the collection of the tax on mulberries (*dout*). Such was the variety of duties and responsibilities of the *hocas* of Algiers.

A second broad group of bureaucrats were the *çavuşes* (Arabic, *sha'ush*). This office, both in the Ottoman system generally and in Algiers, seems to have undergone various modifications. Under the beylerbeys these officials were simply bodyguards, with the rank of sergeant. With the advent of the triennial pashas, they became messengers of state, and the deys employed them as executors of justice. There were sixteen of them, easily identifiable by their costume as they made their rounds in Algiers. Each *çavuş* wore an ankle-length green robe with wide cuffs, belted with a broad crimson sash. On his head he wore a double-pointed cap of white calfskin with the ends folded down over the nape of the neck, and on his feet iron-shod, creased red boots. The *çavuşes* were forbidden beards, but compensated for the absence of that hirsute adornment with enormous moustaches. They were also prohibited from carrying weapons,

53

even so much as a knife. But the respect of Algerine citizens for the office and for Turkish law was such that their orders were instantly obeyed.

The balance of posts in the Algerine civil service consisted of officials having to do with various public and local administrative functions. These included the chief of police (*kikhya el hazinedar*); the director of water services—an important position in an agriculturally disadvantaged region such as Algiers, and held by a *hoca*; the *wardyan başis* (inspectors) of the port and the public baths; the *mizwar* (chief of the morals squad and collector of the prostitution tax); the *muhtasib* (chief supervisor of markets); several *berrahs* (town criers); the *muezzins* (prayer criers); and the *siyas* (public executioners).

A similar efficiency and organizational skill marked local administration in the Algerine state. Algiers had its own mayor and city council (*hakam*), positions which were held by non-Turks as a holdover from the original pact with Baba Aruj. The mayor exercised supervisory legal and police powers over the various craft guilds (*esnafs*) of Algiers, each one answerable to him through its *amin*, or headman. The Algiers urban bureaucracy included such positions as the *caid-el-marsa* (port captain) and the *caid el-fahs*, the chief civilian official of the hinterland of the city. The caid el-fahs was, however, subordinate to the agha of the spahis, the irregular cavalry organized from Berber or Arab tribesmen and maintained on regular pay to supplement the Turkish garrisons.

The Regency was divided into three provinces (*beyliks*)

—Oran, Titteri, and Constantine—and four *caidats*—Blida, Sebwa, Sudan (that is, the eastern Sahara) and El Kala— which depended directly on Algiers. Over-all authority was maintained by the appointment of a bey for each province by the dey. Each spring three separate *mahallas* were mounted by expeditionary forces of the *ocak*, supplemented by spahis and "volunteers" provided by the three beys from their own provincial contingents to show the Algerine flag, collect tribute, distribute presents to the *makhzan* tribes (those whose allegiance to the central government was given in return for local autonomy and exemption from all taxes execpt the tithe, *asir*), and on occasion to invade Morocco or Tunisia as Algerine foreign policy dictated intervention.

Once appointed, and subject to the above limitations, the beys were sovereign in their territories. Each bey's staff consisted of two *khalifas* (one nominated by the dey, the other by himself), a *hazinedar*, and four *çavuşes*. The beys maintained contingents of spahis, whom they furnished with horses and muskets. Janissary garrisons under their orders were stationed in the principal towns in each province. In Constantine beylik there were 300-man garrisons in Bona, Bougie, Collo, Gigeri, Mila, Zemmora, Biskra, Negaous, and Tebessa. Each bey was assigned a permanent honor guard of 100 Janissaries and gunbearers for special occasions, one of whom held the parasol (*dalila*), the ancient symbol of *makhzan* authority in the Maghrib, over his head in his ceremonial parades as he rode slowly through his capital.

Every third year the beys were required to present themselves in person in Algiers, where they paid the tribute and received in return the ceremonial investiture appointment.

55

The pageantry of the Algerine state on such occasions is illustrated in the description by Pananti of the investiture of the Bey of Titteri:

He arrived at the city with çavuşes, gunbearers, spahis and music; on entering the city he scattered gold coins among the crowd. He had with him twenty Barbary steeds; 60,000 riyals bucu (108,000 francs) for the Beytümel *(Public Treasury) and an equal sum for the dignitaries and officials of the Pasha's household. The Pasha received as a special gift 8000 gold riyals bucu in a silken purse. In exchange the bey received, to confirm his appointment, a gold yataghan and a caftan bordered with gold, returning the latter on his departure from Algiers for a fine but less valuable gandourah. He stayed seven days in Algiers, the first four at public expense. Each morning at dawn he called at the homes of members of the divan and the palace. At the end of this period he was safe in the conditions of his appointment and returned to his capital.*

The tribute paid by the beys to the dey of Algiers varied to some extent, depending upon the economic wealth or productivity of their beyliks, and its frequency was also conditioned by their distance from the capital. Thus the sum required of the bey of Titteri was the least—44,000 *riyals bucu* for the *Beytümel* and an equal amount for officials of the government This bey also sent 2,000 *bucu* every quarter to Algiers by courier. Constantine and Oran paid much more. Ordinary tribute for the former was 100,000 *riyals bucu*; in addition the bey provided 50 donkeys, 100 mules, 300 beef cattle, 3,000 sheep, and 20 loads of fine-ground *kuskussu* (semolina wheat) for the government storehouses. Other gifts included hand-woven burnooses, gandourahs, and haiks from the Djerid, where they were loomed of the finest cotton for the wives of Regency officials. The bey of Oran sent an equal amount in tribute along with male and female slaves, red wool burnooses (*filali*), haiks, and horses. Dr. Shaw estimated the total tribute paid by the beys of Oran and Constantine to Algiers at more than three hundred thousand dollars each annually.

The relationship between the beys and the central government mirrored that which existed in the Ottoman Empire. However, the beys were vulnerable to the displeasure of Algiers and could be brought to account by a well-organized *mahalla* if they showed too much independence. On the other hand, the deys in particular found it expedient to grant beylik appointments to *kul oğları*, thus removing from the capital a source of potential subversion. Inasmuch as the beys were also entrusted with the responsibility for defense of the Regency's land frontiers, the forces which they organized for this task represented a counterweight to Algiers. With one or two exceptions, however, the beys remained fully subservient to the Algerine government, the system of collection, tribute and local administration being advantageous to all concerned.

Although Europe saw Algiers as a turbulent state, forever on the brink of anarchy and rebellion, the fact is that during the Regency's three centuries of existence there was not a single large-scale revolt against the central authority. The Turks showed a profound understanding of traditional tribal alliances in the Maghrib. Recruitment of corsairs and military auxiliaries from the indigenous population absorbed rebellious elements, which might otherwise have formed an opposition movement, into the governing structures. Also the state cost little to run owing to the absence of a civil list or high salaries for government officials. Not only were collections for the tribute less as a result, but also loyalty was rewarded with exemption from taxes, noninterference with harvests, and over-all autonomy in local affairs.

A common European criticism of Algiers concerned the instability of the central structure of authority based on the brevity of most reigns, the complete democracy of divan procedure even in matters of state policy, and the abruptness with which deys were replaced. Admittedly the fact that out of twenty-seven deys between 1671 and 1830 only two seem to have lived beyond their term of office—one by abdication, the other in exile—suggests a certain insecurity of position. But the Algerine *government*, apart from its titular leadership, displayed an extraordinary vitality and durability during its existence.

Born amid strife and nurtured by the exertions of adventurers inspired by their faith to drive the Christian Spanish from North Africa, the state required strong management in order to survive. Success confirmed a military tradition among these displaced Turks which became permanent in Algiers, in contrast to Constantinople and other parts of the Ottoman Empire—hence the comment of Dey Ali to Consul Cole, "The Algerines are a company of rogues, and I am their captain." Not even the power and prestige of the Ottoman sultan could shake the hold of the *ocak* on the city they had come to defend and stayed to govern. Thus political leadership in Turkish Algiers became a matter of accommodation. During the period of the beylerbeys, the Ottoman rulers

Süleyman I, Selim II, and Murad III were content to allow an autonomous relationship, and to recall periodically key leaders to Constantinople to be rewarded with high office in the Ottoman government itself. The pattern was established with the appointment of Kheireddin, and was continued by such notable Algerine figures in the sixteenth century Mediterranean wars as Salah Reis, Uluç Ali, and Hassan Veneziano, all of whom, like Kheireddin, were former corsair captains.

In 1568, following the death of Uluç Ali, Murad III issued a firman abolishing the separate title of beylerbey (although Ottoman dispatches continued to refer to *Cezayir beylerbeyisi* on into the nineteenth century) and replaced it with the office of pasha as the ranking official of Algiers. Pashas were appointed by the Porte for three-year terms. A further element of stability was provided by the fact that a number of pashas served more than one term. Pasha Khizr, first appointed in 1588, held the office four times; Köse Mustafa, three; and several pashas, two.

With the passage of time and continued naval success, Algiers became increasingly self-sufficient and disinclined to honor the authority of the Porte in the appointment of pashas. Although they were received with full ceremony, the appointees found themselves isolated, unable to develop an effective base of support outside the *ocak* because of the rule excluding nonethnic Turks from command and the absolute control exercised by the soldiery over internal affairs. The corsairs, because of their frequent absences from Algiers, could not be counted on to buttress the pasha's position. Furthermore, they were just as concerned as was the *ocak* with the preservation of their rights and privileges.

The line of Constantinople-appointed pashas came to an end in 1658–59 when Pasha Ibrahim, serving his second tour of duty, utilized the confusion following the bombardment of the city by Admiral Blake's squadron to impose a tax on the annual subsidy sent to the corsair *reisi* from Constantinople. This action caused a riot, whereupon the Divan abolished the pashalik in favor of a government of the aghas of the *ocak*. There was, thereafter, continuous friction between the corsairs and the *ocak*.

The first three aghas—Khalil, Ramazan, and Ibrahim—were murdered after they tried to extend their one-year assignments. Subsequently, Şaban Agha negotiated a truce between the two factions and governed until 1664, followed by Agha Ali until 1667, as Algiers reverted to the system of triennial rule established by the Ottoman sultans. Agha Ismail succeeded him, but his apparent weakness in the face of French demands for the restitution of prisoners from Provence and recognition of French rights over the town of Dunkirk motivated a revolt, and Ismail was executed in 1671. The corsairs took advantage of the situation to vest authority in a dey (literally, "uncle"), a title corresponding to the commander of the army in Tunis at the time, and elected one Haci Mehmed as their candidate. From this period on the office of dey, sometimes called pasha-dey, was in effect in Algiers. As European resistance to the corsairs grew firmer and better organized, the *taife* relinquished its privilege of nominating deys to the officers of the Divan, and Algiers became for all practical purposes two republics—a land-based *ocak* and a self-contained guild of corsair sea captains.

Any regularly enrolled member of the *ocak* was eligible

for the office of dey. Election of this office was accomplished with absolute equality and by unanimous vote. On the death of the ruling dey, the Divan would assemble and his demise would be announced by the *berrahs* through the streets. All members of the *ocak* would then leave their barracks and proceed to the dey's palace to vote for a new candidate, each one shouting aloud his choice for the position. If a candidate did not receive unanimous support, he would be excluded, and other candidates offered to the ballot until one of them had received the unanimous support of the *ocak*. When this happened, the successful candidate was obliged to accept his appointment. He was seated on the throne of his predecessor, and servants wrapped him in the ermine-trimmed caftan symbolic of the office. The *ocak* then saluted him, crying, "We consent; be it so; God send him prosperity," and filed from the room. The grand mufti of Algiers then read aloud the list of obligations of the office, observing that, God having called that particular dey to lead the republic, his authority should be used to execute impartial justice, ensure internal security, generate necessary revenue, and provide regular pay for the soldiers. The new dey then kissed the hands of the mufti and of other dignitaries present, while outside the palace frequent salvos of cannon announced the change of masters to the citizenry of Algiers.

Since the Regency did not observe any legitimate law of succession, the election of each dey was considered to require confirmation from the sultan. An envoy was sent to Constantinople immediately following election to request such confirmation. The requests were invariably honored, and in each case a *kapici başī* (messenger of state) proceeded to Algiers with a copy of the confirming firman along with the red caftan of honor and saber of state which served as the sultan's official recognition of the office. From the period of Ali Çavuş (1710–17) onward the deys were given the rank of Pasha of Three Horsetails in the Ottoman army.

The firman of investiture sent to Algiers by Mahmud I in 1746, following the election of Ibrahim Hoca as dey, provides us with an excellent example of the style and terminology of these confirmatory documents. The relevant passages are as follows:

... it is an absolute duty of Our august Person, that the floods of Our generosity and kindness wash over all men, and principally over the noble government of the Illustrious Pasha, guardian of the frontiers of Islam. The Regency of Algiers is one of the countries held in Our hands as a trophy of the brilliant victories of Our magnanimous ancestors who sleep now in Paradise—May God's light shine on them— This country is in the forefront of Islamic states and its valorous inhabitants are the foremost champions of the house of faith and defenders of the true religion and the unity of the One God. Thus, ever since the equitable reigns of Our illustrious predecessors until this glorious epoch of Our august Caliphate, all requests of the Algerines have been favorable received, all their wishes graciously welcomed by the sovereigns of Our dynasty; it is unnecessary to state that the people of this Regency have been at all times the enemies of the enemies of Our Sublime Porte; that to earn Our Imperial pleasure, source of all goodness, has been their first wish, and that they have always demanded from Our hands the investiture of authority. Under these circumstances We have been informed in an official report ... that the former Governor

*and Dey of Algiers, Ibrahim Pasha, has just passed away,
and that his nephew and lieutenant, one of the ranking
officers of the Regency, . . . the possessor of this imperial
tughra as of today, Ibrahim Hoca, had been nominated by
the unanimous consent of the Chiefs of the Regency and all
those who have the right to take part in these deliberations.*

*But the nomination and dispatch of the Deys of Algiers
being done ordinarily by Our Sublime Porte, conforming to
ancient custom, as the Chiefs of Algiers in their general
petition, and Ibrahim Hoca in a private request, have today
made supplication, as a mark of Our sovereign grace and
Imperial favor We graciously deign to confer on the aforesaid
Ibrahim Hoca the worthy appointment of Governor and Dey
of the Regency.*

The informality with which deys were chosen or elevated
from the ranks gave rise sometimes to unexpected twists of
fortune. Certainly the most unusual elevation was that of
Baba Mohammed ben-Osman, (1766–90), the longest-reign-
ing and most effective of Algerine rulers. He came from a
small village in the vilayet of Karaman in southern Anatolia,
where he had been recruited for the *ocak*, at an early age and
taken to Algiers. There he married, had a son, and was
subsequently, for unknown reasons, castrated. That ended
his military career. Undaunted, he apprenticed himself to a
shoemaker, and then opened his own shop where he made,
sold, and repaired shoes for his former comrades in arms. He
not only prospered but won the respect of all for his industry,
humility, and honesty. One day a *çavuş* came looking for
another Mohammad, also a shoemaker, who had been rec-
ommended for the then-vacant post of babī hocayī (hoca of

the gate). By mistake he called at the shop of Mohammed of Karaman and gave him the post. From then on Baba Mohammed's star brightened as he rose steadily through the administrative ranks to become eventually *hazinedar* and then dey. Yet his humility and awareness of his good fortune never deserted him. "It was written," he said of his accession to the highest post. He died in his bed, peacefully, and the succession passed without incident to his son Hassan.

The deys' prerogatives as heads of state included the general administration of justice, the declaration of wars, the signing of peace treaties, and the renewal, or rejection, of concessions such as those granted to the Compagnie Lenche for coral exploitation in the offshore banks of the Bastion de France. The deys also convened meetings of the Divan, received tax collections and tributes from various European powers as well as their own beys, and appointed officials to the various posts comprising the central government. Their term of office was originally intended to be six months, but this limitation proved impractical due to the length of time required to obtain the firman and accompanying symbols of investiture from Constantinople. Factional disputes within the *ocak* and the insistence on unanimity before a candidate could be elected made the life of a dey hazardous. Haci Ṣaban Dey (1689–95), who was much admired by British Consul Cole for his "joyous demeanor, prompt and decisive character," was murdered by the soldiers on September 10, 1695, in the midst of a Divan meeting, and Dey Ahmed once commented to a visitor that "I have to do with such unruly fellows that what I eat at night I forget in the morning!"

Nevertheless, the tenure and the performance in office of many Algerine sovereigns compare favorably with those of

European rulers during the same period. Next to the twenty-four-year reign of Baba Mohammed, the longest reigns were those of Baba Ibrahim (1732–45), Hűseyin (Hussein), the last dey(1818–30), and Haci Mohammed (1671–81). The average reign was six years long and in the context of Ottoman administrative practice represented a continuation of the earlier system of appointment of pashas for three-year terms. Furthermore, the co-ordination of Ottoman and Algerine foreign policies toward Europe was maintained continuously until 1830 to mutual advantage, quite apart from the professions of allegiance with which the Regency's leaders signified their attachment to the sultan-caliph of Islam. If his throne of bricks and marble rested on uncertain underpinnings, each dey of Algiers appeared to the external world —and particularly to the European consuls and negotiators who dealt with him—as the visible symbol of an opulent and powerful state. Thus Joel Barlow, U.S. consul to Algiers from 1795 to 1797, described Dey Sidi Hassan (1790–98) following an interview:

. . . his feet [were] shod with buskins bound upon his legs with diamond buttons in loops of pearl; round his waist was a broad sash glittering with jewels, to which was suspended a broad scimitar, its sheath of the finest velvet. In his sash were stuck a poignard and a pair of pistols, said to have been a present from the late unfortunate Louis XVI; the dagger was of pure gold. Upon the Dey's head was a turban with the point erect, which is stylistically peculiar to the royal family. A large diamond crescent shone conspicuously in the front, and on the back of which a socket received the quills of two large ostrich feathers. . . .

IV

THE WEB OF ALGERINE SOCIETY

The social structure of the Regency reflected the diverse
ethnic origins and backgrounds of its citizens, with the presence of the Turks supplying an important leaven to the established cultural mix. The over-all population remained constant at approximately 200,000 (estimates for Algiers range
from 100,000 to 130,000 out of this total) for the period of
Turkish rule. This mix may be broken down for the sake
of convenience into four broad social categories: Turks,
Maghribis (including the *kul oğlari*), renegade Christians,
and Jews.

Apart from a common interest in the defense of their
portion of the Ottoman Empire against Europeans—mani-
fested in such acts as the contribution of a day's free labor by

each occupational guild to repair of Algiers' defenses—the main characteristic of these four groups was their social harmony. A high degree of social cohesion was achieved under the authority of the *ocak*, while the elite status of the Turks reinforced the respect for Turkish law and order instilled in the mass of the people by the Barbarossas. As a result, the Regency was domestically tranquil, and Algiers became one of the most orderly and well-policed ports on the Mediterranean, a place where Christian ships from nations at peace with the Regency could find safer anchorage than in many of their own harbors.

The internal stability of the Algerine state and its Turkish identification encouraged the development of cultural and social links with the eastern portions of the Ottoman Empire despite the distance of Algiers from the rest of the empire. In this respect the Regency compares favorably with the early Ottoman principality of Sultans Osman and Orhan centered in Bursa. Both states were built upon stable social foundations, the principal difference between them being that the early Ottomans were concerned with the establishment of an individual state within the Islamic community, whereas the Algerines were an Islamic bastion facing a hostile Christian world. But similar social factors operated in Algiers as in Bursa. The merit factor provided a strong inducement to the captured Christian to apostasize; once he had done so, the renegade could enter government service and aspire to all but the very highest positions. The over-all status of the Christian renegades seems to have been better than that of the non-Turkish Muslim population of Algiers. A third factor, exclusion of the *kul oğlari* from the *ocak*, served to minimize social friction at leadership levels. A fourth, the establishment of a self-policing authority of Janissaries under their superiors, while the rest of the Muslim population was answerable both to Shari'a law and to civil regulations, established acceptable definitions for intergroup behavior.

One of the positive developments of Turkish rule in Algiers was the reduction of traditional factionalism in the central Maghrib. The ancient distrust between rural and urban areas, with consequent isolation of the city from its natural hinterland, broke down. Consequently Algiers, and to a lesser extent cities like Constantine and Tlemcen, resumed the roles of economic, intellectual, and cultural centers which they had played in Roman days. At the same time the political acumen of the Turks in governing by accommodation with local or tribal authorities altered forever the old image of the North African city as a source of political repression. This accommodation was effected by certain social assignments which were differentiated from the governmental assignments described in Chapter III. For example, the monopoly on street-maintenance jobs in Algiers was held by Biskris, swarthy Berbers from the region around Biskra at the edge of the Algerian Sahara. Other (blind) Biskris were employed as guardians of the gates to the various quarters of Algiers, which they closed and locked at night.

An even more formalized arrangement was made with the Mzabites, descendants of the Ibadi Kharijite refugees who had established a theocratic league of cities deep in the Sahara in the tenth century, after being expelled by the Fatimids from the central Maghrib. The rigid Hanbalism of the Mzabites found an answering echo in Turkish orthodoxy. Their theocracy was respected, and they were allowed to maintain an *emin* (trustee) in Algiers with the right to civil jurisdiction over them on behalf of their *kadi* resident in Ghardaia, with their Ibadi rite recognized as the legitimate mark of a millet. Mzabites in Algiers monopolized the positions of hammam attendants and formed the majority of butchers and millers. Kabyles, Banu Abbas, Shawia, and others from the rough Maghribi tribes flocked to the cities of the Regency with the establishment of "Ottoman peace" to seek employment as tailors, shepherds, unskilled laborers, and domestic servants in a sort of preindustrial urban migration.

Jews formed the only recognized non-Muslim millet. The innate scorn of the Turks for their Muslim subjects did not extend to the Jews, whom they regarded with a certain superstition as having access to black magic and the occult in money matters. During the period of the deys, Jews were employed to transact much of the commercial business of the state, and to conduct negotiations with European merchants which involved a knowledge of languages and Mediterranean commercial transactions beyond the capacity of the Algerine rulers. This arrangement, initially a marriage of convenience, led in the nineteenth century to the monopoly on Regency foreign trade by the Busnach and Bacri families which was to prove the downfall of the Algerine state.

The Jews were seldom persecuted. A pogrom threatened by the dey in 1690 because of allegations that they had stolen a Christian child for the ritual Passover sacrifice was averted by a substantial contribution to the *Beytümel*. The Jews were, however, set apart in dress and residence from their neighbors. The male Jew wore "drawers not to hinder him in making water, a Waistcoat of wide sleeves so as not to hinder washing to the elbow, a broad Girdle with goodly great Knives in a sheath on the left hand; breeches in winter like

the Spaniards; zapatas or coloured shoes to put on and off
without touch of the hand; a kind of gown uppermost." Like
Muslims, Jews always wore a head covering, usually a turban
or a skullcap. Jewish women seem to have been permitted
somewhat more public freedom than their sisters in Islam,
which they indulged in, Gramaye tells us, by sitting at their
doors "on Mats or Carpets, prating all day long, except when
they go to the Baths, Hermits, Wizards, Sepulchres, Gardens
and Feasts common with them . . . and have little care of
their Children."

Both Ottoman and Anatolian Turkish influences affected
Algerine society in a variety of ways. The official language of
the Regency was Osmanli Turkish, itself a fusion of Arabic,
Persian, and Turkish words written in Arabic script and
extremely difficult to translate. The flow of recruits for the
ocak from Anatolia brought another, rougher form of Turkish into North Africa. Because Algiers' military-naval vocation dominated its commercial life (as distinct from Tunis),
the Turkish linguistic contributions emphasized the military;
out of 634 words of Turkish origin used today in Algeria, 72
are military in nature. Arabic, because it was the language
linking the tribes of the interior, urbanites whose residence
predated the Turkish conquest, and Spanish Morisco refugees, remained in common use. The presence of renegades,
prisoners in large numbers, and resident European merchants
gave rise to a lingua franca called *Franco* or *Sabir* (from the
Spanish verb "to know"), which combined Arabic, Spanish,
Turkish, Italian, and Provençal terms and was the medium
of communication in Algiers.

In dress, home furnishings, domestic pursuits, music, and
other diversions the Algerines emulated the society of Otto-

man Constantinople. Despite their considerable distance and cultural remoteness from the Ottoman capital, they seem to have regarded themselves as an outpost of Ottoman culture in the Maghrib. Yet they were justly proud of their role as the principal Muslim maritime power in the Mediterranean, equal to any coalition of forces Europe could bring to bear on them. The elaborate costume of the ruling Algerine officials, which was duplicated on a lesser scale down the line of the elite to the lowest member of the *ocak*, refined Ottoman tastes on Maghribi models. The traditional man's costume of North Africa, an ankle-length seamless cloak with wide sleeves and sometimes a hood called a jellaba in Morocco, jibba in Tunis, and burnoose in Algeria, was supplemented with more elaborate underpinnings. Men of quality wore two or three vests, open at the throat, ornamented with buttons, lace trim, and embroidery; wide, baggy, calf-length trousers of muslin or white cotton; babouches; and either a turban or a red *sheshia*. The trousers were belted with a broad silk sash in which the wearer stuck his pistols, yataghan and dagger. Concealed in the scarf were his silk money purse, Venetian watch, and any other personal possessions. This costume was sufficiently distinctive to be known to Mediterranean travelers as the "Algerine style."

The seventeenth and eighteenth centuries saw a blend of Levantine Arab, Turkish, and Maghribi styles into an urban costume appropriate to the stature and wealth of the corsair state. This costume consisted of wide, pleated cotton trousers and a sleeveless linen shirt; a *sedria*, a short jacket of wool or linen with sleeves but no cuffs; a caftan in a solid color, usually red or blue, without a collar and open in front, decorated with buttons and sometimes trimmed with fur;

and to complete the ensemble a *ferja*, a floor-length, swirling cape cut in a circle. In the eighteenth and early nineteenth centuries the caftan came to be reserved for officials and was replaced for others by two or three embroidered Ottoman-style vests. The babouches with turned-up toes brought from Levant and copied by Algiers' several thousand cobblers became the fashion in footgear.

Changes in the Ottoman military structure initiated by Selim III with his *nizam-i cedid* (new order) and completed by Mahmud II in the early 1800's motivated some "modernization" in *ocak* costume. Tarboosh or fez replaced the pointed cap and turban. The caftan was belted to provide a carrying place for yataghan and pistols and the babouches began to be worn over soft leather boots. Apparently there were no restrictions on color combinations other than the use of black, which was reserved for Jews as the only permissible color for their outer garments and was their badge of identification.

The non-Turkish Algerines, except for Jews, were more simply clad—a linen shirt; knee-length pleated trousers; then in winter the *ghlila*, a knee-length cassock; followed by a *dorra'a*, a very long robe of fine linen; and to complete the ensemble a burnoose. Merchants affected more elegance. Their group status was marked by embroidered slippers with a raised iron heelplate and a red cloth skullcap wrapped with a thin cotton band in the manner of a turban. In this respect the social-occupational trademarks which distinguished traditional North Africa were given added emphasis by the Turks in their zeal to set themselves apart as a ruling class, providing a thin but viable thread for Muslims to grasp when the flood of French civilization poured over their land.

Outside of the cities of the Regency and especialy among

the tribesmen, Turkish influences were considerably less. As he had for centuries, the tribesman wore little more than a white woolen cloth five to six feet long and nine wide called variously haik or gandurah, wrapped and draped around the body and belted with a cord, and covered by a burnoose. Tribal leaders, sheikhs, members of the ulema, and officials appointed by the Turks wore as a mark of their status a small scarlet cap, actually a turban of wool bands decorated with figures and smybols; the order and number of the bands indicated the rank and occupation of the wearer.

As might be expected from the position of Algiers as a part of the Ottoman dominions and a unit of the Islamic community, women occupied a secondary role in the predominantly masculine Algerine society. There were no heroines of the stature of Dido, Sophonisba, or El-Kahina, the Judaized high priestess who led the Berber resistance to Islam. Aside from the obvious fact that the corsair profession by its nature excluded women, the masculine confraternity of the *ocak* was a further deterrent to the influence of women in the affairs of the military republic. Also the rulers, being products of an unstable electoral system in which their elevation was frequently challenged, were unable to develop the protective harem system which insulated the Ottoman sultans from revolt but at the same time exposed them to harem intrigue and indirectly to female domination. As a result, Algerine women represented in an absolute sense the domestic side of Islamic social existence; they were the literal hearth (*ocak*) which Algerine arms and ships defended.

Country peasant women, according to Shaw, appeared in

a haik, under which a shirt and pantaloons were worn, the

upper part of the haik being converted into a species of sack, for the purpose of carrying the youngest children; the head is covered with a handkerchief interwoven with gold and silver threads; worn with it is a triangular piece of linen, embroidered and colored with considerable art, which hangs down the back.

Urban ladies pursued a more elaborate toilette and, perhaps owning to the isolation of their lives, were strongly influenced by Constantinople fashions, which were brought to Algiers via emissaries returning from missions to the Ottoman capital. The wives of maried Turks wore commonly the *farmla* (*fermele*), a decolleté corset or girdle, one or more long-skirted vests with short sleeves and/or underskirts over these loose trousers, when at home. When they went out in public, they put on three layers of embroidered capes, knee-length and belted with a wide embroidered sash, then long baggy trousers, square-toed slippers, and over all a white haik; their faces were veiled to the eyes with a semitransparent white handkerchief.

The hair was the principal beauty feature, most admired when it fell to the feet. The construction of the *sarma*, the distinctive Algerine headdress, occupied many hours. Once the hair had been brushed, combed, plaited, and perfumed with musk or *nessari* rose water (the finest essence), it was gathered into a chignon and bound with a gold or silver band, twelve inches wide, which rested on the part down the back of the head. A second band, richly filigreed, was bound around the first so as to enclose all the hair in the form of a cone, while a transparent band of gauze embroidered with trailing colored ribbons completed the creation. The *sarma* clearly resembled the hennin of Elizabethan England and required the same proud carriage affected by English court ladies.

Algerine women were very fond of perfumes, ornaments, and cosmetics. Eyebrows were heavily darkened with kohl, whether naturally dark or not, while the fingertips, palms, and soles of the feet were stained with henna. The eyebrow was arched in the shape of a crescent, a symbol of special significance to Turks as well as Muslims. The inside corner of each arch was then extended to join above the bridge of the nose and a small figure such as a dot or pear designed just above the linkage. Sometimes the eyes were encircled with black lead. Another mark of beauty highly prized among the *kadinlar Cezayirli* (women of Algiers) was gazelles' eyes (i.e., large, limpid, and brown). If a lady's eyes did not measure up, walnuts were boiled, dried, and powdered; the powder was then mixed with water to form a liquid paste which was spread over the eyebrows with a lead comb and drawn gently down over the eyelids with a silver needle. A liberal application of rouge and a beauty spot completed the make up.

One a week, the Algerine ladies went to the hammam. This event represented not only a ritual purification but also a kind of fashion show along with the traditional exchanges of family news. On such occasions the family wealth went on display. The bourgeoises of Algiers might wear heavy bands of gold around wrists and ankles, and crescent-shaped earrings often five inches in circumference and as long as a man's little finger dangled from their ears. To carry such heavy earrings, the female ear was perforated in several places, and a small roll of paper passed through each hole until it had been enlarged enough to allow the passage of a date pit. Pearls and coral—the latter brought from the coral fisheries near Bona—were also popular; they were worn in strands around the neck. A common piece of jewelry was a single pearl or gold ball on the end of a heavy golden chain, a symbol of the dependence (which for Europeans meant slavery) of the woman on her husband.

The veil, which apparently had been in sporadic use at most among North African women in the early years of the Regency, had become a necessary article of exterior clothing by 1780. It was of two kinds, the small half-face "mask" mentioned above and a cloth fringe stitched to the haik itself. Venture de Paradis described the veiled *Algeriennes* abroad as so many Grecian goddesses in their floating silk or linen robes, one hand held at the chin to keep the veil in place.

Embroidery and other forms of needlework were the principal activities of the women of Algiers. Embroiderers specialized in curtains, headdresses, and kerchiefs, although the embroidering of caftans and other articles of clothing, male as well as female, occupied many hours of work and produced a highly artistic product. In motifs and style Algerine curtains resembled those of Anatolia and the Levant, with improvements due to better dyes and the instinctive skill derived through generations of craftmanship. The characteristic symbols were the pomegranate and the artichoke, both typical of Turkish woven fabrics. The usual colors were red, blue, and mauve, the latter probably identical with the "Tyrian purple" used in Roman royal robes. Algerine door curtains, which were used in lieu of solid doors in the interior passages, and between rooms, usually consisted of three horizontal bands. The needlepoint technique used was known as "Turkish point," and the embroidery, featuring eyelet stitches instead of the standard brick stitch, was referred to as *zelilec*, or "Turkish stitch."

Ottoman influences were felt in other areas of cultural life in Algiers. With the advent of corsair wealth it became common practice to build town houses *à la Turque*, with a large waiting room at the entrance, leading into a central courtyard with galleries along each of the long sides which opened off into small shallow rooms. The furnishings of low tables, cushions, and small chests embossed in mother of pearl or ivory were of the sort found throughout the Ottoman lands, and frequent addition of European porcelain, marble, mirrors, silks, and velvet hangings acquired through captured prizes replaced a certain ostentatious charm by mere clutter. The floors were covered with either Anatolian prayer carpets or with gay Turkish kilims, which were carried from room to room as the need arose. These carpets, plus the large platters of beaten red copper set on wooden bases called *sini* and carved with characteristic Turkish motifs added Turkish touches to Algerine home decoration. So did the coffeepot (*kahvetyere*), always called by its Turkish name. New Janissaries often brought them in their gear, and the retired members of the *ocak* gave them as *evkaf* for the collective use of new residents of the barracks when they left the service.

The architecture of public buildings also reflected Turkish models. Thus the mosque built in 1622 by an Italian renegade reis, Picenino (who took the name Ali Biçnin (or Biçnur), had an octagonal cupola set on a central arcaded square courtyard, with smaller octagonal cupolas serving as the roofs of the arcades. In 1696 Dey Ahmed ordered a modification of the kubbe of Sidi Abd al-Rahman al-Tha'alibi

77

(died 1470), the principal marabout of Algiers, to convert it into a funerary mosque by the replacement of the traditional Hispano-Moorish dome with a similar cupola. The most striking example of the use of Ottoman-Anatolian models was found in the Fishery Mosque (1660), built by the *ocak* as a center for the Hanafi rite from funds from the *seboul-kheirat evkaf*. (irrevocable trust). Its dome was loftier than other Algerine mosques. It was suspended on pillars and was shaped upwards to meet the convergence point of four naves which formed a sort of cradle, flanked by four octagonal cupolas at the angles. The same design is found in the Kilise Cami in Constantinople (Istanbul). The small walled grave-yards (also an Anatolian feature) adjoining each of these Algerine mosques also reflected Turkish influences in funer-ary decorations; their carvers made extensive use of the four basic Turkish floral elements, the eglantine, the tulip, the jasmine, and the daisy.

The daily pleasures of the table, weekly baths, family visits, periodic marriages or funerals, rare ambulatory enter-tainment or festival, and obligations of the faith marked the social life of the Regency. The ordinary citizens were rela-tively little affected by the factional conflicts erupting within the government, or by the occasional naval bombardment; they simply closed their shops and doors until the storm had passed. The return of corsair vessels with their prizes punctu-ated their existence with considerable spectacle, but it too was of a transitory nature.

A number of Turkish dishes became standard fare in the Regency alongside the traditional North African *kuskussu*. Pilaf (pilau or pilaw), a staple diet in Anatolia, was also common fare in Algiers. The Algerines made much use of *dolmas* (literally, "stuffed") of various kinds, such as *sovan dolmasī* (onions filled with minced lamb and rice), *yaprak dolmasī* (meat wrapped in grape leaves), and so on. *Kebabs* (cabobs) of beef, lamb, or mutton were common on Algerine dining platters, as were *köfte* (meal balls cooked in various ways), a popular item today on Turkish menus. A variation on the *kebabs* called *makarun* was described as follows by William Davies:

> [*It is*] *a paste made of sugar and water, of which they take a bit as big as a bean, and put it in the middle of a wire, rolling it in their hand till it be two or three inches long, then boil it in water with three or four whole onions, and when in the dish, mix it with grated cheese and pour butter on it; they usually eat quick and having done everyone returns thanks saying* Hamdulilla!

The hammams of Algiers had important social purposes apart from their hygienic function. (As noted earlier, the sources of water for the capital were sufficient to provide running water and/or bathtubs for a large percentage of city homes; the hammam was where Algerines became ritually as well as hygienically clean.) Here, urban men and women met in their separate suites or rooms; here marriages were arranged or initiated, funerals were discussed, business deals brought to the coffeehouse stage, and family events narrated among friends. The hammams, of which there were about sixty in Haedo's day, were large, clean buildings, lighted at the top, and provided with hot and cold water. The bather entered, paid his two *bucu*, left his clothes in a large outer room, and passed naked into another large room divided into cubicles able to hold ten to twelve persons. In each cubicle hot water passing through bronze pipes set in the walls generated clouds of steam. The bather passed through progressively hotter steam rooms until he reached the *sicak odasi*, the "calidarium" of the Romans. There he stretched out on long velvet cushions, surrounded by clouds of hot incense-laden steam, and contemplated the mysteries of life. After he had rested in this soporific state for a few minutes, two burly *hizmetcis* (literally, "servants") appeared, stretched his limbs until all the joints had been made to crack, rolled him about like kneaded bread, and scraped him with coarse fingerless gloves to remove what appeared to be more than a pound of flesh. This done, the bather returned to his dressing room by the same route, drank a glass of sherbet provided him by another attendant, was sprayed with rose water by a third, put on his clothes, and departed, with his blood circulating with unusual celerity, while a general feeling of animation spread through the whole system which seemed to give it new life and activity.

The women's baths were similar to those of the men, but the ceremony was more elaborate, the customers having more time on their hands and fewer opportunities to consort with friends. After the ladies had completed the various stages of the steam bath itself, female *hizmetcis* washed them from head to foot in rose water and sprayed them with musk and other perfumes. Their eyebrows were then tinted, and they put on their clothes, which had previously been hung over a brazier containing a fire of aloe wood. In the dressing room, not only sherbet but also candied fruit, nuts, and other delicacies awaited them, including the Turkish favorite, *lukum*, a kind of marzipan. Music and dancing girls were also provided by the establishment, and in this agreeable fashion one day a week passed for Algerine ladies.

As was true elsewhere in the Islamic world, marriage in Algiers was an important institution, combining elements of entertainment, politics (at least where important families were concerned), social behavior and status, tradition, and even economics, as well as the continuity of lineage decreed by clan or tribe. Polygamy was apparently no more common in the Regency than in other regions of the empire and perhaps less so because of the presence of the masculine confraternities of *ocak* and corsairs. Sometimes the ships that brought recruits to Algiers for the *ocak* also conveyed Turkish women, although the far more common miscegenation of Turk and native Maghribi is attested to by the number of *kul oğları* and the absence of social prejudice, as opposed to political exclusion, for them. Among the Algerine bourgeoisie, apart from the occasional imposed demands from rulers or high officials on private citizens for their daughters as a consequence of some special act of protection or exemption from taxes or service, marriage was an affair arranged between families, conducted with elaborate negotiations and strict ritual, and intended to last.

A common feature of the marital institution in Algiers was the go-between, usually an elderly woman friend of the family of either the prospective bride or the groom. Algerine girls were nubile by the age of twelve or thirteen, and in view of the public secrecy enveloping females, go-betweens performed a valuable function. They might go from house to house on missions for families with eligible sons and inquire as to the presence of marriageable females, or alternately bring news from time to time of the physical development of the girls of one household to parents desirous of contracting marriage for their son. Go-betweens were equally useful in providing fathers with economic information concerning their prospective in-laws.

Algerine marriage ceremonies varied according to the financial circumstances of the families, the social groups involved, and as might be expected the urban-rural differentiation. Among the Kabyles the act of consecration was simply a matter of the bride and groom holding each a cup to the other's lips in the presence of witnesses. Pananti observed the elaborate preparations for the marriage of an urban *haute bourgeoisie* couple in Algiers, which lasted over several days:

A few days before the celebration the groom goes about the town to the sound of drums and fifes ... on the wedding day he takes another round, covered by a red cloak with a fine sabre by his side. There is also a veil thrown over his face to prevent the operation of the evil eye. For three consecutive days the bride is conducted to the hamman, until the marriage takes place. On that occasion relatives and friends being assembled, the husband repeats a prayer before them, and then proceeds to join the bride in her apartment; they are now declared man and wife by means of certain prayers recited by the husband and Imams. ...

As was the case in Algerine weddings, the bride then removed her veil and her husband now saw her unmasked for the first time. The groom then retired to his residence, to which the bride was conveyed on horseback, riding in an enclosed palanquin and accompanied by friends waving lighted torches as well as strolling flautists and drummers and being carried through her husband's door, "great care being taken that she does not touch the threshold, this being considered a bad omen," she was received into her new home.

Algerine weddings were occasions not only for families to show off their wealth or display for their daughters a magnificent dowry (*ceyiz*), but also for extraordinary efforts at female adornment. Elizabeth Broughton records in her *Six Years Residence in Algiers* her mother's attendance at the wedding of the daughter of the kadi of Algiers to an elderly, one-eyed Turk, and notes that when the *sarma* of the bride was finished it was so heavy that she was unable to walk across the room unsupported. Instead of a bouquet, she carried a wreath of purple crepe studded with pearls. The couple then plighted their troth in rose water, which an attendant poured from a silver ewer into their cupped hands and each in turn drank from the palms of the other.

Such were the principal elements in the Algerine marital institution. Turkish sobriety and respect for the literal requirements of Islamic law placed great store on female virginity, its proof being contingent on final acceptance by her husband of the bride, and sexual misbehavior as well as incidence of intercourse among the religious communities was extremely rare. United States Consul Barlow, in a letter to his wife in 1796, observed that "if a woman is taken in adultery the law condemns her to be placed in a large sack with a stone and thrown into the sea. . . . sometimes the husband asks and receives permission to take the law into his own hands."

Fear of such brutal punishment on the part of potential transgressors, however, was less a deterrent than the more positive presence in Algiers of formalized prostitution. Although it was rumored that members of the *ocak* were fonder of young boys, particularly Jews, than of young women and would often abduct them, the only positive records we have are those of the corps of non-Turkish prostitutes maintained for the pleasure of celibate *yoldaşlar*. They were under the supervision of the mizwar and were strictly controlled, inspected regularly, and required to live in a special urban quarter which was barred and locked to outsiders. Before he could visit this quarter a prospective client had to submit a request to the mizwar stating the price he could pay and the day he wished to enter; he was then issued an authorization. The arrangement was similar to that of the *Kafes* (Cages) existing in Constantinople. Algerine prostitutes were employees of the state; they paid taxes on their earnings and performed a useful service in a tough, albeit law-abiding, community.

A number of other social diversions and activities reflected the important Turkish influence on Algerine life. Algerine festivals were called *bayrams*, from the Turkish word for religious holiday, and naturally the principal ones were associated with the socioreligious procedure of Islam. The major festival was *Kurban Bayrami*, or *Büyük Bayrami* (literally, Muslim Great Festival of Sacrifice), which corresponded to the *'Id al-Adha*, or *'Id al-Kabir*, of the Arabic-speaking Islamic world and celebrated the ritual sacrifice by Abraham of a ram in place of his son Isaac. Other festivals were *Şeker Bayrami* (Festival of Sugar, so called because of the exchange of gifts and small cakes of sugar) on the occasion of the end of the Ramadan month of fasting, and *Mevlid-i-Şerif*, the birthday of the Prophet Muhammad.

The public observance of *Kurban Bayrami* was borrowed

from the Ottomans. Once the *müftü* (judge) of Algiers had determined through comparison of a black and a white thread that the new day had indeed dawned, the guns of Algiers boomed, and the ruling dey repaired to his lionskin throne to receive the congratulations and gifts of members of his government and of representatives of foreign governments resident in the capital. The sovereign then led a procession of dignitaries, townspeople, and the membership of the *ocak* to the Fishery Mosque, where the ritual sacrifice of the ram took place, while the guns continued to boom and a military band played martial music. After the formal prayer service was over, the gates of the dey's palace were thrown open to the public and an elaborate *kuskussu* served to everyone present.

Algerine music was primarily military in nature, reflecting its Ottoman origins. The *ocak* military band consisted of twenty-seven pieces: eight large drums called *davul*, played with the fingers; five kettledrums (*nakkare*); ten bugles; two trumpets; and two pairs of cymbals. The type of music was *mehter*, a strongly accented rhythmic style popularized in the Ottoman Empire by the Janissary corps and synonymous with Ottoman military pomp and power. A second popular type of music was the Andalusian, brought by Morisco refugees from Spain and incorporating the use of such Oriental instruments as the *'oud, tar, rebeb* (a two-stringed violin), and *ney* (a reed flute) featured in Anatolian Mevlevi dervish compositions, on a semitonal scale. During the period of the Regency, Andalusian orchestras of twenty or thirty persons could often be heard in Algerine cafés, "playing all by ear, and hastening to pass the time quickly from one measure to another, yet all the while with the greatest uniformity and exactness, during a whole night," as Renaudot tells us.

Along with *mehter* music, two other distinctive Ottoman forms of entertainment became popular in Algiers. These were *Karagöz*, a form of puppet theater, and *gureş*, or greased wrestling. *Karagöz* ("Black Eyes" in Turkish) was the central figure in the shadow theater, which may have originated in China or India and was carried westward by the Turkish tribes, perhaps to be merged with similar types of the genre developing in Egypt and the Near East. The Turkish version supposedly arose in Bursa, during the reign of Orhan, the second Ottoman sultan, who had ordered a mosque to be built. Among the workmen on the project were a certain blacksmith named Karagöz and a stonemason named Hacivat. They were very droll men, so much so that all work on the mosque ceased as the other workmen crowded around to listen to their conversation. There are a number of versions as to what happened next, but the most common one is that Orhan became very angry and ordered the two to be hanged.

Later one of his courtiers came to him and repeated some of the conversations. The sultan was filled with remorse at what he had done, and to console him the retainer, Şeyh Küsteri, built a screen and manipulated puppets representing the two dead humorists behind it. Gradually a repertoire of dialogues and supplementary characters evolved, and the *Karagöz* figures (one-dimensional puppets carved from transparent leather, moved by rods, and joined with string, and presented behind an illuminated screen) represented the principal form of popular entertainment from Oran to the Zagros Mountains of Iran. The substance of their dialogues ranged from off-color jokes to political satire and imitations of high officials, in performances sometimes given in private homes, sometimes in cafés, all the better to delight the rough-and-ready and irreverent soldiery of Algiers.

Greased wrestling was equally popular among the male citizens of the Regency. The Algerine wrestling champions (*pehlivans*) were local heroes, and bouts between them were featured at the various *bayrams*. On these occasions eight to ten *pehlivans* were paired off in twos, and were then rubbed with olive oil until their skins shone and they had become slipperier than eels. Wearing nothing but oiled leather shorts, each pair then preceeded to wrestle to a fall. Less formal *gureş* bouts were also held regularly on Fridays at the Bab el-Oued, just after the noon prayer service. Dr. Shaw described one such contest as follows:

Anon, there comes one boldly in, and strips all to his drawers. Having done this, he turns his back to the ring and his face towards his clothes on the ground. He then pitches on his right knee, and throws abroad his arms three times, clapping his hands together as often, just above the ground; which having done, he puts the back of his hand to the ground, and then kisses his fingers, and puts them to his forehead; then makes two or three good springs into the middle of the ring, and there he stands with his left hand to his left ear, and his right hand to his left elbow; in this posture and the challenger stands, not looking about, till some one comes into the ring to take him up; and he that comes to take him up does the very same postures, and then stands by the side of him, in the manner aforesaid. Then the trier of the play comes behind the pilewans, *. . . and covers their naked backs and heads and makes a short harangue to the spectators.*

After this the pilewans *face each other, and then both at once slap their hands on their thighs, then clap them together, and then lift them up as high as their shoulders, and cause the palms of their hands to meet and with the same, dash their heads one against another three times, so hard that many times the blood runs down. This being done, they walk off from one another, and traverse their ground, eyeing each other like two game cocks. If either of them finds his hands moist, he rubs them on the ground, for the better hold fasts and they will make an offer of closing twice or thrice before they do. They will come as often within five or six yards one of the other, and clap their hands to each other, and then put forward the left leg, bowing their body, and leaning with the left elbow on the left knee, for a little while, looking one at the other just like two fighting cocks. Then they walk a turn again; then at it they go; and as they are naked to the middle, so there is but little holdfast. . . . He that throws the other goes round the ring, taking money of many that give it him. . . . Having gone the round, he goes to the tryer, and delivers him the money so collected, who in a short time returns it again to the conqueror, and makes a short speech of thanks. While this is doing two others come into the ring to wrestle.*

The social exercise of religion was profound in Algiers. Islam pervaded every aspect of existence for the Algerine people from birth to death. William Davies noted:

The Turks are very zealous in their religion. . . . A Turk will keep his word if he swears by his head, putting his hand upon his forehead. . . . The manner of their churches is this— the church is very fair within, with many hundreds of lamps

*burning, all matted underfoot, without any kind of picture
or seat. . . . In the morning at the top of the church they hang
out a white flag, and in the afternoon a blue one, for a sign of
their coming to church, then goeth eight or ten of them to
very top and cry out with a loud voice.*

Turkish zeal and the superstition of an unlettered military elite gave rise to such religious-related customs as turn-
ing one's back to the sun when stopping in the street, being
seated at meals with the left foot under the right, toes to the
east, and so on. Belief in evil spirits (*cin taifesi*) and the
interventionary powers of marabouts was strong. The marabouts had a special role as intercessors and devotional objects
for Algerine women, since they were not permitted to participate in public prayers. Women visited in the kubbes regularly
to make votive offerings, light oil lamps, and lay flowers in
support of the divine intervention they sought to alleviate
social or family difficulties.

The round of death evoked a similar response. It began,
as Gramaye tells us, "When any is sick, women assist women
and men the men, praying eastward; (if these unsuccessful,
and the sick person dieth) the women wash the body with
hot water and soap, clothe it and carry it, with the Caid's
leave, with the head forward to burial; if death be on Friday
it stayeth the prayer time in the mosque." The corpse was
then accompanied to the graveside by the majority of the
congregation, chanting Koranic suras and walking rapidly
"so the angel of justice might not be delayed in receiving the
soul of the deceased." Once arrived at the site, which was
either *evkaf* land or an area set aside by common consent for
the purpose, hence sanctified, the body was interred in its

coffin in the family plot. A stone was placed at the head and another at the feet, each inscribed with Koranic verses; men's gravestones were marked by a turban, women's by garlands of flowers.

Mourning was especially protracted for women, who were required to spend part of the next eight days at the grave, chanting and recalling the good qualities of the deceased, and thereafter to go every Friday as part of the obligatory service of the Muslim Sabbath. Male members of the house did not shave for three days after the funeral, and "no fire is allowed in their house, nor anything boyled." The women wore black for the same period, and thereafter were exempted from this habit, except that a widow of a man of social standing would remove her rings for a white ribbon and wear purposely soiled clothes. Widows were considered to be in mourning for four months and ten days, after which they carried baskets of combs and fresh eggs to the seaside, offering the eggs to the first passerby, who could not refuse. The act released them from their affliction (Pananti) and they could remarry.

The ultimate effectiveness of any social system rests on the operation of its laws, and in this respect the Regency of Algiers represents a considerable achievement. The prior history of a region as large as all of western Europe, in which no indigenous central government had ever existed, and the fact that the state was fashioned by Turkish adventurers uniting a population bred of lawlessness give the achievement a rare significance. The explanation lies in the absolute fidelity of the Turks to the laws of Islam, the self-policing nature of the *ocak*, the impartial nature of Algerine justice, and the limits set on punitive measures. Furthermore, learning and education were equated with the law, and it was assumed that offices of legal authority were held by those most deserving of them. The remission placed on Jews, who were left to the jurisdiction of their own magistrates, and on non-apostate Christians also made the operation of the legal system much easier.

There were in effect two Islamic legal systems in Algiers, one based on Hanafi jurisprudence for the Turks, and another drawn from Maliki prescripts for the rest of the Muslim population. Each had its own kadi, who in the early seventeenth century was sent to the Regency from Constantinople. The kadi was the lowest judge of appeal in all cases except for members of the *ocak*, who could appeal his decisions to their agha. The second echelon of justice was occupied by the *müftüler* (singular, *müfti* or *müftü*). They were nominated by the dey, on the basis of their honesty and learning, and could be identified by their snow-white caftans. The imams, the lowest level in the religious establishment, had no legal responsibilities, but were frequently called upon to render opinions in cases where Koranic precedents were contradictory or unclear.

An accused person had the right of sanctuary in mosques or the kubbes of marabouts, but this could be circumvented by building a wall around the place of refuge until the escapee either surrendered or starved to death. The law applied equally to all persons; unless the evidence of guilt was clear and the crime obvious, an impartial trial was guaranteed. Cases were heard daily except Friday by the respective kadis, with the help of notaries; the *müftüler* held their sessions twice a week (Shaler). The proceedings were taken down in either Turkish or Arabic, depending on the system involved and the participants. The parties pled their cases themselves, the use of lawyers being unknown, but were allowed to use witnesses for verification of facts and as character references. In the occasional situation involving both jurisdictions, the Turk could appeal to his own kadi or *müftü* if dissatisfied with the verdict; otherwise, the two jurisdictions were exactly equal.

Justice was swift and summary as well as impartial. Trials rarely lasted more than several hours. Sentences were not recorded by name but by a seal or ocher stamp which the presiding kadi placed on whatever record of testimony had been made. Adultery (which was extremely rare) was punished by the drowning of both parties. Murderers were sentenced to death. Thieves had the right hand severed and then slung over their shoulders; they were then placed on a donkey and led around the city, facing backwards and preceded by a bailiff crying, "Thus are thieves punished." (Pananti). For forgery the sentence was the same. The punishment for sedition, conspiracy, or fraud was strangulation or hanging. Debtors were imprisoned until all their property had been sold; if this were more than sufficient to meet the debt, the surplus was returned to the prisoner; if not, he was released anyway and could not be placed in double jeopardy. But he had to serve a 101-day sentence and receive a bastinado of 100 strokes in any case.

The death sentence was carried out in one of three ways (Davies): ganching (impalement), the stake, or beating. Observed Davies:

Ganching is after this manner—he sitteth upon a wall, being five fathoms high; under the place where he sits is a strong

*iron hook fastened, being very sharp; then is he thrust off
the wall upon this hook, and there hangeth sometimes two
or three days before he dieth. Staking to death is thus: a
round piece of wood, three yards long, as big as a man's leg,
sharp at one end, is driven in at the buttocks of the offender
and out at his shoulder, and so they let him die till he bee
dead.... The manner of beating to death is thus—they take
the offender and lay him down upon his back, being naked,
and with two double ropes two several men beat on his belly
till he be dead.*

"However," adds the writer, "these deaths are very seldom
used because they are so fearful to the offenders."

Far more common was the use of the bastinado; the
offender was upended and beaten lightly but steadily on the
soles of his feet or the buttocks with small sticks, the size and
thickness of a finger, the number of strokes being from fifty
to a thousand according to the nature of the crime, after
which vinegar would be poured over his wounds.

Three other aspects of Algerine law are worthy of note.
The first of these was the application of the system to the
ocak. Not only were its members subject to the exclusive
jurisdiction of their Hanafi law, but also the law was applied
to them out of sight. Although a Turk might misbehave in
public, his examination and sentencing were applied *in
camera*. This arrangement may have contributed to the
seditious ambitions and general turbulence of the Janissaries
as far as the government was concerned, but it gave the public
a feeling of confidence in the establishment's regard for public order, as well as a belief that the *ocak* would curb the
excesses of its own members.

The other elements in the legal system of the Regency which made it work were the thoroughness of enforcement and the application of collective responsibility. Thus, in one case (Renaudot), a Christian prisoner was caught in a house of ill fame with a Muslim who had befriended him and brought him there. The Christian was adjudged guilty because he had violated the statutes governing prostitution (Christians were forbidden to enter the brothels), the Muslim was equally guilty because he had furnished the pretext, while the three prostitutes who had received them were given fines and jail sentences. Another case, though fictional, as recounted by Underhill in his *Algerine Captive*, provides an excellent example of the working of Algerine justice:

The Kadi sat on a cushion crosslegged with a slave holding a whip and batten on one side, and another with a drawn scimitar on the other. The Plaintiff had bought a mule which appeared sound but proved to be blind and lame. Witnesses were called who confirmed the contract between the two men and testified as to the defects of the mule.

The defendant admitted his guilt, but said that four years earlier the plaintiff had sold him a broken-winded camel, and he had been waiting all this time to get revenge. Witnesses were called who confirmed this testimony.

The Kadi rendered judgment as follows: the defendant received fifty strokes of the bastinado; the plaintiff received fifty blows for his first cheat; the parties were dismissed without costs; an officer of the court was ordered to sell the mule at auction and distribute the proceeds to the poor; lastly, as one witness was believed to have given perjured testimony, he received fifty blows of the batten, was mounted on the

mule facing backwards and led through the city, where at
every corner he was ordered to stop and shout—"Before the
enlightened and just and merciful Kadi, Mir Karsan, in the
trial of Osman Bekr and Abu Is'ul, I spake as I ride."

Algerine justice rested on the principle of collective
responsibility supplementing the efficient internal security
forces. Each quarter for the cities and each rural district were
made responsible for robberies committed within their limits.
Food prices were state-controlled, and part of the dey's oath
when he was sworn in had to do with the maintenance of
price regulations. Some of the deys took this obligation literally; Dey Ibrahim once went to a shop disguised as a servant
to verify a rumor that the shopkeeper was selling bread and
rice at prices above the legal ceiling, and brought the man
immediately to trial when the truth was discovered. On another occasion, Ṣaban Dey observed a corsair at a Divan
hiding something under his burnoose. When he asked the
corsair what he had hidden, the man produced some plums,
which he said he had bought from a merchant of Marseille.
Said the dey, "If you can afford such fine fruit, you must have
stolen them, for otherwise you would have bought bread for
your family in preference; you deserve a hundred strokes of
the bastinado for having made your family suffer merely to
gratify your own gluttony." Then the merchant was sent for,
and recognized the corsair's basket of plums as one stolen
from him, whereupon five hundred lashes were added to the
sentence for the theft and for having told a lie about it.

The deys' vigilance, lastly was supplemented by their
police organization. Police patrols circulated in the cities at
stated intervals, while a special "flying squad" of a police
officer, patrolmen, and the public executioner patrolled day

and night on a flexible schedule to watch for violations of moral or legal behavior. The *mizwar*, due to his supervisory responsibilities for prostitutes and for one of Algiers' three jails, had to be on the alert all through the night, and was required to submit a report to the dey every morning describing the activities of the previous night. In this fashion law and order governed behavior in Algiers so thoroughly that internal dissidence never reached even an embryo stage in the three hundred years of Turkish rule.

V

RESOURCES AND REVENUES

Although throughout the Mediterranean world the Algerine state was identified with the efficient conduct of warfare by a ruthless military government. Algerine power rested on secure economic foundations. The natural resources of the state were managed in such a way as to preserve the mercantile system which had created for Algiers a stable balance of trade and adequate production in pre-Turkish days. Three additional sources of revenue were generated by the corsair campaigns—prizes and cargoes, European payments of tribute, and the Ottoman subsidies—while there was a continuation of legitimate commerce carried on by Regency ports as outlets for the products of the hinterland.

Important as these revenues were in the rise of Algiers

to first rank in the Mediterranean, they were grafted upon a sound and productive agriculture. Turkish rule was designed to maintain rather than to overburden the existing system; conversely, the French conquest with its ensuing flood of landless European settlers and its unenlightened protection-ism, was equally well calculated to destroy that system. Within the restrictions imposed by climate, fertility, and limited resources, land-use patterns in the Regency were effective and production sufficient to meet the needs of the population. The "unexploited stagnation" ascribed to Otto-man Algiers by such French authors of a later era as Boyer (*Alger à la Veille de l'Intervention Française*) fails to take into account the industry and zeal of Algerine proprietors, both Turkish and indigenous Muslims. The conversion of Algeria into a debtor colony, with its entire economy mort-gaged to the metropole, was not their doing, but would be left to the accomplishment of France.

The flourishing state of Algerine agriculture prior to the conquest was attested to by many observers. Haedo, on being taken outside of Algiers on one occasion, commented on "the infinite number of gardens and vineyards filled with lemon orange and lime trees, flowers of every kind, and fountains of clear water, which runs through all parts in abundance." Shaler writes of his visit to a suburban region that "the soil has not degenerated from its ancient fertility, being in some parts black, in others red, but everywhere being strongly impregnated with nitre and salt." Much as they are today, the hills encircling the capital were dotted with villas built by merchants and corsair captains; Renaudot noted in 1830 that the trees in many of their orchards bore two, sometimes three, crops annually due to the rich soil and the care of their owners. The skill of the Turks as cultivators, evidenced in the fruits and vegetables of Anatolia, was supplemented by that of Christian captives whose agricultural competence had been established before their purchase; their owners installed them permanently in their country houses, where they tended gardens and orchards on a year-round basis.

Perhaps the best example of Algerine productivity under Turkish rule was the Mitidja. This region lying to the south and southeast of Algiers, described by French botanist Desfontaines, in 1784, as "overhung with pestilential airs and laced by stagnant waters forming unhealthful swamps," and cited as the major reclamation area of the French colonists, was already being extensively cultivated in the 1600's by Algerine proprietors. Elizabeth Broughton, in her journal, *Six Years Residence in Algiers*, mentions in the course of one excursion a place "which we surnamed the Valley of Asparagus, from its sandy soil being entirely covered with that delicious vegetable, far surpassing in flavor any in France or England and quite as large as those usually sold in the streets of Paris." Michael Russell in his *History . . . of the Barbary States* writes of the Mitidja, "It is fifty miles long by twenty broad, and everywhere watered by numerous springs and rivulets."

The difference between the Mitidja in Turkish times and during the century of French rule was primarily one of type of cultivation. The former presented a more or less typical pastoral-agricultural appearance, with numerous small white villas set amid gardens which grew truck crops and were self-sufficient, lanes bordered with Barbary fig and aloe, orchards, flocks of chickens, livestock, and many mills wherein the grain destined for Algerine cities was ground. In the

99

latter period the small farms gave way to huge estates, each one dominated by its red-tile-roofed manor house, and devoted to citrus and viniculture.

Yet Algerian viniculture did not originate with the French *grands propriétaires*. The small vineyards which were—and are—a common feature of Thrace, the Turkish Aegean coast, and other suitable regions of the eastern Ottoman dominions were a familiar sight in the Mitidja, the Oranais, and the lower slopes of Kabylia. Turkish viniculture was practical, efficient, and successful. In February the vineyards were thoroughly weeded and all grass was removed. The vines were then left alone until April, when they were pruned down to the main trunk or stem. With no further care, they promptly grew back vigorously, with the harvest coming in late July. Bunches weighing as much as fifteen pounds were not uncommon, with grapes three to four inches in circumference.

Until the late seventeenth century the crop was destined to be table grapes and to be processed into vinegar. Increased contact with Europe and the broadening of taste among the upper classes in Algiers led to the production of Algerine wine, which was bottled and sometimes drunk locally, although the greater part was exported for European tables. Algerine wine up until 1723–24 was considered fully equal to the best that Europe could produce. In that year a plague of locusts wiped out the vineyards, and the quality of the product thereafter was regarded as being equal to French *vin ordinaire*, but no better. Thus the agricultural productivity of French Algeria, far from being an original achievement, was a case of expansion of a well-established local industry.

The administrative decentralization of the Regency encouraged the development of secondary ports and cities along with their agricultural hinterlands, although Algiers remained the chief port and center of economic activity. Constantine was second in importance, although situated two hundred miles from the coast. Its importance grew originally in part out of its impregnable position astride a deep gorge raised above the surrounding plains, but equally to its location in the center of the stock-raising High Plains. The finest Barbary horses were bred in this region, from which they were exported to European markets via the ports of Collo and Bougie. Oran (despite changing hands several times until the final retrocession from Spain in 1792), and Bona also experienced a steady growth under the stabilizing authority of the *ocak*. Bona was the major outlet for the leather, wool, butter, and dates of Kabylia, giving the Kabyles a dependable market for the produce of their small mountainside farms. Nicolay provides a vivid description of Kabylian agricultural progress under the Turks, in contrast to the depressed and impoverished state reached by the region through the "civilizing authority" of France. He writes:

Bona hath a fair and sumptuous mosque, deep cisterns rather than fountains and wells without the city a goodly and large Champion Country which beside the great quantitie of Corne that it bringeth forth, nourisheth Oxen, Kine, sheepe and other Cattel, so pleasantly that with their milke and butter not only the citie of Bona is provided but also Tunis and the Isle of Jerba.

Bougie, thirty leagues east of Algiers, was another valuable link in the commercial and agricultural production chain of the Algerine state. A significant local trade in tools and utensils fashioned from iron quarried from the mountains around the city and eastward into Kabylia was carried on there, mainly for local use, but with some export to other parts of the Ottoman Empire because of the high quality of Algerian iron ore. Bougie was also a principal source of the olive oil, wax, and honey exported from the Regency to eastern Mediterranean ports.

Both agricultural and mineral resources were well distributed throughout the Regency. The principal iron ore and lead deposits were located in Kabylia. There were also extensive deposits of pipe clay, fluorides, and rock salt, the last being mined primarily for sale to the nomadic tribes of the Sahara. The iron ore of Kabylia was of particularly high grade; however, exploitation was for domestic use rather than export. The one mineral resource which was of interest to external developers was coral, and there was intense competition among European states for the concession, which was eventually acquired by the Compagnie Lenche and resulted in the establishment of the Bastion de France.

Inland Algeria was devoted to pastoralism to a much greater extent than later under French rule. The traditional authority of tribal chiefs over the economic activities and internal affairs of the pastoral tribes was respected by the Turks, and this "Pax Turcica," which served the region better than the Pax Romana because of the religious bond, encouraged the growth of large-scale stockbreeding, for export as well as domestic use. The Algerine tribes raised both fat-tailed sheep (karakul) as well as straight-tailed ones, along with goats, camels, and Barbary horses. Tribesmen rarely slaughtered their animals, but sold those not used for dairying purposes at town auction markets—a system still in use in Algeria and its Maghribi neighbors.

Barbary horses were an important export. Fine stallions frequently figured among the gifts of Algerine sovereigns to Christian princes and were an essential part of the tribute of beys to the deys. The Barbary camel, originally brought from Egypt by the mysterious people known to Herodotus as the Garamantes, became the key to survival for the tribes of the Sahara. The peoples of North Africa held this animal in great veneration, washing themselves in the desert with camels' spittle and often referring to the camel as Hajji Baba, "Father of Pilgrims," because of the custom of Islamic rulers of sending presents to Mecca on the occasion of the Grand Pilgrimage on the back of camels. The trans-Saharan commerce which linked Algiers, Tunis, and lesser African Mediterranean ports with West African cities such as Gao, Kano, and Timbuktu depended on camels for transportation. Camel caravans gliding through the desert at the rate of some two and one-half miles an hour for fifteen or sixteen hours per day were welcomed on arrival with their cargoes of gold dust, ostrich feathers, dates, and a not inconsiderable number of black slaves destined as unskilled labor in Algerine cities or as servants in Algerine upper-class households.

Wheat was an important Algerine crop. The hard variety was the only one grown in the Regency. Sowing took place usually in the middle of October, after the onset of the autumn rains, with the harvest coming in late May or early June; the crop was considered safe if the spring rains fell on schedule in April. The sources differ as whether one or two harvests yearly were obtained by Algerine farmers (Shaw states categorically that there was only one), but all agree as to the productivity. Two and one-half bushels were sufficient to sow an acre of ground, the ordinary yield being from eight to twelve. Certain areas performed even better; the Marwani variety, grown in the "Algerine breadbasket" around Midi-yah, averaged fifty grains per stalk. The Regency produced in most years a surplus sufficient for export; in the first half of the eighteenth century Englsh factors resident in Oran shipped between seven and eight thousand tons of wheat annually from that port to England.

Apart from the special revenues obtained from its function as a corsair state, and the collection of taxes, the Regency derived considerable revenue from legitimate commerce. Its principal exports, to Europe and the eastern provinces of the Ottoman Empire in the eighteenth century, for example, were carpets, embroidered handkerchiefs, silk scarves, ostrich feathers, wax, wool, animal hides and skins, dates, and a coarse native linen similar to muslin. Shipments of this last item, interestingly, were fashioned into a finer product in the German city of Osnabrück and in the early nineteenth century found great popularity in the United States. The American purchasers of this cloth called it *Osnaburgh*, from its place of export, not realizing that it had been furnished to its German exporters by the cloth merchants of Algiers.

The Regency in turn imported a variety of products from abroad. These included, *inter alia*, raw and spun cotton, damask linens, gold and silver stuffs, frankincense, playing cards, combs, spices such as anise and cumin, and cosmetic items such as cochineal and vermilion. Algiers was not an active participant in the trans-Saharan slave trade, but there was a modest traffic in black Africans, one hundred and fifty to one hundred and eighty individuals annually who were purchased as house servants for fifty to one hundred and fifty sequins each by the wealthier Algerine families. These servants were treated more leniently than Christian prisoners. They were frequently allowed to purchase their freedom and were sometimes manumitted by their owners. In both cases they were then regarded as full citizens of the state.

Algiers dominated the production of certain items fabricated in the Maghrib. One of these was the *sheshia*, the round knitted cap popular with young Muslims in the Levant as well as North Africa. Algerine shawls and burnooses, both of silk and wool, found a ready market because of their quality and the fact that Algerine cloth held dyes well. Palm-leaf baskets from the Chott Djerid and rush mats woven by the Banu Abbas tribe were also popular in the Islamic world. Last but most celebrated was the attar of roses distilled from Algerine bushes, the finest brand being the *nessari*, an essence distilled from the white rose of Blida.

The main obstacle to the expansion of legitimate Algerine commerce arose from the periodic imposition of monopolies by the state in order to collect guaranteed revenues. Salt was a national monopoly and could not be exported, while the exportation of olive oil and of dressed hides was permissible only within the Ottoman Empire. The bey of Oran, for an annual payment of fifteen thousand dollars, was granted a monopoly over the total export trade of his beylik. The French, in addition to the coral concession, paid thirty thousand dollars a year for the right to control the exports of Bona, which included wool, hides, wax, and sixteen thousand quintals of wheat. These restrictions discouraged local economic development although contributing an element of economic stability to the Algerine state. Algiers also required the issuance of special licenses for exports of grain and live-stock. The rights to export hides, wax, and raw wool were also granted as annual concessions to the highest bidder. As a result of these various restrictions, Algerine commerce frequently showed an unfavorable balance of trade. The consular report of William Shaler for 1822 gives the balance shown in the table on the opposite page.

The most important point to be noted about Algerine legitimate commerce, apart from its relative unimportance in the growth of the state, is that its modest size and prospects, along with the lack of interest in commercial or industrial expansion on the part of the rulers, discouraged the over-spending and economic commitments to European interests which undermined the Ottoman Empire elsewhere. In theory the deys subscribed to the Capitulations, but in practice Algerine commerce was subject to local ordinances, which were scrupulously applied. The import duty on all items was 12.5 per cent, and on exports, 2.5 per cent. A port charge of twenty dollars (Spanish) was also levied for anchorage in any of the ports or bays of the state.

Speculation in any of the imports considered to be essential in the defense of Algiers, such as lumber, wrought-iron hardware, cannon, small arms, and naval stores, was prohibited. A similar probity and strictness regulated the trans-Saharan trade conducted on behalf of the Algerines with the market towns of sub-Saharan West Africa by cara-vans originating mainly in Ghadames, on the Libyan border. Once he had reached a town such as Kano or Zaria, the caravan merchant would unload at a certain spot the wares (Turkish daggers, scissors, beads, salt) brought down from Algiers. The prospective African buyer would then place

Imports

Source of Origin	Commodities	Value ($ Spanish)
England	Manufactured goods	500,000
Italy (Livorno)	Silks, brocades, sugar, pepper, coffee	300,000
Italy (Genoa)	Manufactured goods	
France	Sugar, coffee, pepper, steel	200,000
Ottoman Levant ports	Raw silk, finished cloth	100,000
France, Italy	Diamonds, silver plate, lumber, unset gems	100,000
Total		$1,200,000

Exports from All Algerine Ports to Marseille, Livorno, and Genoa

Quantity (Quintals)	Commodities	Value ($ Spanish)
20,000	Wool*	160,000
10,000	Hides*	80,000
600	Wax†	18,000
-----	Ostrich feathers, miscellaneous articles	15,000
Total		$273,000

*Average $8 a quinta.
†Average $30 a quintal.

beside the pile the amount of gold dust and/or ostrich feathers which he considered to be equal in value to the Algerine shipment. Both parties then withdrew, the merchant returning separately to remove the payment, if satisfied, or to reclaim the shipment, if not. In the latter case the African buyer would add gold dust to the pile until both sides were satisfied.

Aside from its maritime and trans-Saharan trade, Algiers derived important revenues from other sources: taxes, the dey's one-fifth share in corsair acquisitions, the European tribute, *awad* (gifts to the rulers on special occasions such as the end of Ramadan from the representatives of foreign powers), trade concessions, and the financial contribution of the Porte to the *ocak*. The principal taxes were the *asir*, a tithe paid in silver on all products of the soil; the *haki* (or *tapu*), a tax on tenants of makhzan lands, paid at a fixed rate per plough used, plus labor charges; a head tax on Jews; and the *lazma*, a similar levy imposed on nomadic tribesmen, residents of oases, and on those farmers resident in Kabylia whose lands were not subject to measured ploughing. The property of persons dying intestate or childless also reverted to the state. Apart from the tribute paid by the beys, there were various autonomous districts, notably Kabylia, which were permitted local self-government under their tribal sheikhs and assemblies in return for contributions to the national treasury.

As of the mid-eighteenth century, these various taxes produced revenue of three hundred thousand Spanish dollars annually, with an equivalent amount derived from corsair prize sharing, intestate property, and the Kabyle contributions. United States Consul Shaler computed the receipts of the *Beytümel* in 1822 as follows:

An Account of the Receipts into the Treasury in 1822
(in Spanish Dollars)

From the Bey of Oran, a tax assessed upon that province	$ 60,000
From the same, for the franchise for exportation from Oran	15,000
From the Bey of Constantine, a tax assessed upon that province	60,000
From seven Kaids dependent upon the general government, assessed	16,000
From the Bet el Mel, or judge of inheritances, an assessed tax	40,000
From the Scheich [Sheikh] el Belled, an assessed tax	3,000
From the Bey of Titterie, a tax assessed upon that province	4,000
From the Khodgia of hides, a tax assessed upon his office	4,000
From the Khodgia of the custom-house, the same	800
From the Jewish nation, an assessed tax	6,000
From the custom on importations	20,000
From the rents of the national domain in the city of Algiers	40,000
	$268,800

European tribute payments for the same period were:

Accounts brought up	26,800
From the government of France for the monopoly of the coral fishing at Bona	30,000
From shipment of wood, wax, and hides	40,000
Tribute paid annually by the king of Naples	24,000
,, ,, ,, by the king of Sweden	24,000
,, ,, ,, by the king of Denmark	24,000
,, ,, ,, by the king of Portugal	24,000
	$192,800

Besides the above, the Regency also receives annually as a tax from various Arab Scheichs two hundred thousand measures of wheat and from the Beys of Constantine and Oran, ten thousand measures of barley each, which serve for the subsistence of the seamen, soldiers, and labourers in the public service.

Public expenditures were as follows:

An Account of the Public Expenditure of the Regency in the year 1822

Annual expense of labourers, artificers, &c. in the dock-yards	24,000
Annual purchase of timber, cordage, and other stores for naval purposes	60,000
Annual pay of navy officers and enrolled seamen	75,000
Annual pay of the military of all classes	700,000
	$859,000

It should be noted that the deficit indicated in the budget shown above is not an accurate reflection of the economic status of Algiers, since it is based on European computations. In its financial transactions and monetary system the Algerine state was part of the Ottoman Empire and functioned as such. An Ottoman mint was located in Algiers, and Algerine currency was minted in conformity with the metal content, values, and weights set by official Constantinople standards. In the reign of Sultan Mahmud II (1808–29) both gold and silver coins were issued. The gold coins, called *sultani*, were actually worth more than their Constaninople equivalents. They were of three types: *sultani* (3.200 grams),

half *sultani* (1.650 grams), and quarter *sultani* (0.800 grams).
They were struck with the inscription "*Duru fi be Cezayir*"
on one side and "*Sultan Mahmud Han Azze Nasara*" on the
other. These large circular coins were designed with considerable artistry, and because of their value and gold content
there were not many in circulation.

Silver was the main medium of Algerine currency. Algerine silver coins were also very artistic and minted of pure
alloy; the silver content was very high. The basic unit of
value was the *bucu*, also called the *riyal bucu*, weighing ten
grams. (*Bucu* means "to mint" or "to circulate.") The coin
in commonest use and employed in most commercial transactions was the *zevc bucu* (double *bucu*); it is the piece
called by Europeans the piaster of Algiers and by the Arabic-
speaking peoples of the Ottoman Empire *duru Cezayir*, to
distinguish it from the *douro Español* of intra-Mediterranean trade. These double *bucus* bore the same inscription on
one side as the *sultanis*, with the date of minting rather than
the year of reign; these reverse image was inscribed "*Sultan
ul berreyn ve hakan ul bahreyn essultan Mahmud Han azze
nasara.*" Other *bucu* denominations were the *rabi*, equal to
one-quarter of a *bucu*, and the *sümün*, one-eighth of a *bucu*.

For accounting purposes these coins were divided into
units called *mevzune* (variously *messoon, mesonne, mesom*,
in European accounts), valued at one twenty-fourth of a
bucu. The *mevzune* was not a coin of Algiers, but it was
equivalent to a small, blank oval silver piece issued in Marrakesh, Morocco; sixty such units equaled one Spanish dollar in
commercial accounts. The Algiers mint issued four small
coins, of either pure copper or copper alloy, to represent
fractional values of the *mevzune*. The smallest coin of all was

the *akçe*, an irregular shaped, roughly square coin inscribed only with the word Allah; it was the asper, or aspre, of European accounts. As noted earlier, with the French capture of Algiers the Algerine mint was shifted to Constantine, where Bey Ahmed continued to issue coins with Mahmud's monogram and the inscription "*duru fi be Konstantiye*" until 1847, when the city fell to a French expedition.

From an economic standpoint, of course, the domination of Algiers over its Mediterranean neighbors, Christian and Muslim alike, was derived from the revenue-producing activities of its corsair fleet. A comparison with the beylical state of Tunis serves to illustrate the distinction. Tunis, far more advantageously located than Algiers to conduct trade with both eastern and western Mediterranean ports as well as Europe, possessed of a superb natural harbor, and the natural outlet for the agricultural produce of a well-developed hinterland, never reached the political heights attained by Algiers. The wealth amassed by the Algerine corsair captains equaled if not surpassed that of the *beledi* (native) merchants of Tunis. In this context the contribution of the corsairs to the Algerine economy was outrageously effective.

Corsair revenues which reverted to the state were drawn from three principal sources: the cargoes of prizes taken at sea, the ransom of captives, and tribute paid by various European nations under formalized treaty arrangements to protect their ships from corsair seizure. A fourth source of income was derived from the marine establishment itself through dockage permits, fees for refitting and repair of visiting squadrons, and the value of the fleet and shipyard.

The sale and distribution of Christian captives formed

the largest part of corsair revenues in Algiers, both from their initial price and through the funds provided for their later ransom. Although referred to as "slaves" by all European sources, captives in Algiers, as in all Ottoman territories, who were not Muslims were considered as *tutsaklar,* "captives of war," or *kullar,* "creatures of God's property," rather than *esir,* "slaves," the term applied to Black Africans who were sold by the slave traders in the North African markets. The captive was an item of property; once sold, a title deed to him was registered at the Treasury and conveyed to his owner by the *hoca el-pencik.*

Captives not selected by the dey to serve as pages or servants or bought by individual purchasers became the property of the state. They were used for work in quarries, along the roads of the Regency, on state farms (*miri*), or in the Algiers arsenal and shipyard. When not working, they were lodged in bagnios, large buildings similar to the Janissary barracks. If a prisoner had a particular trade, he could hire out to a merchant or shopkeeper and retain up to one-third of his earnings. Women captives of quality, assuming they appeared to have the resources to obtain their ransom, were lodged in the mansion of the Sheikh el-Belediye pending ransom arrangements. Less fortunate ones, of whom there were few, were sold at auction along with the men. There was a brisk prisoners' brokerage in Algiers on the expectation that a small investment would later bring a huge profit, since many prisoners changed owners several times before they were ransomed.

The peak period for acquisition of captives was in the early sixteenth century, Algiers' finest era, when the corsairs ranged almost unopposed through the western Mediterranean and as far north as the English Channel. Gramaye gives statistics for the years 1607–18 (excluding 1615):

1607	3 towns Calabria attacked		1400	captives
1608	42	ships captured	860	"
1609	36	" "	632	"
1610	23	" "	384	"
1611	20	" "	464	"
1612	3,804	captives from Spain		
1613	16	ships captured	230	"
1614	35	" "	467	"
1616	34	" "	767	"
1617	26	" "	1763	"
1618	19	" "	1468	"

The principal duty of European consuls was the direct ransom of prisoners or intervention with the Algerine authorities on behalf of their captured countrymen. In this humanitarian effort they were assisted by members of religious orders such as the Trinitarian Fathers, the Jesuits, and various Protestant denominations who were sent on missions to Algiers for this specific purpose. Unfortunately, much of our knowledge of Algiers is derived from the mission reports of such liberators, who in their concern for the religious deprivation of their parishioners ignored the fact that captives of the state were reasonably well housed, paid a regular wage, and given the use of a chapel and the run of the city except at night.

The procedure for ransoming a prisoner by a religious order was fixed and absolutely impartial. Upon arrival in Algiers, the emissary presented himself to the port authorities, stated how much money he had brought with him, and paid 3.5 per cent of this sum as a sort of port duty. In addition, he presented an equal sum in the form of gifts to the dey and representative of the Divan. He was then provided with lodging and an interpreter and allowed to notify his church (or mission, if one was in operation in the city). The prisoners whom he had come to ransom were brought from their various residences, by their owners, or from the bagnio, in order of their length of stay, the longest first, and allowed to contribute whatever savings they had amassed toward the ransom money. The amount of ransom was set by the dey. When the ransom had been paid, the prisoner was handed over to the emissary and given a white cloak in token of his redemption. The priest or churchman then led all the redeemed prisoners to the *belediye* (city hall), where the attestation of freedom was issued to him for each captive. The emissary then took formal leave of the dey and led his little procession to the harbor to debark. An additional 10 per cent was levied on the total ransom amount before the prisoners were allowed to take their long-desired leave of Algiers.

Occasionally bad relations between European consuls and the deys worked hardships on the prisoners. The Dey Ibrahim, angered over the insistence of the French and Spanish consuls that prisoners be repatriated under the terms of the peace treaty between Algiers, Spain, and France, in 1731, ordered all captives chained, flogged, and sent to hard labor in the Algiers quarries until a higher ransom was agreed on. But such mistreatment as a mark of official policy was rare.

Captives, then, were regarded as a source of revenue rather than objects of exploitation per se in Algiers. They were neither more, nor less, mistreated than any other component of the Algerine labor force. They had one advantage over Muslims captured by European corsairs (for these existed, particularly in Calabria) or by the warships of Christian nations, in that they seldom served as oarsmen on the galleys of the *reisi*. Galley service was an honor reserved in Algiers for freeborn Muslims, although the corsair ranks were enlarged by many renegade Christians who added their seafaring skills to those possessed by Muslim captains. The steady decline in the numbers of captives, from thirty-five thousand in the mid-seventeenth century to two thousand in the 1790's and twelve hundred in 1800, also lessened the intensity of crusading fervor with which Europe regarded Algiers. What had once seemed a brutal form of human debasement, a vivid reminder of the barbarity of Algiers, gradually assumed the more normal proportions of a logical policy of economic realism which, although unjustifiable in human terms, could be understood by their adversaries as the best the Algerines could do in the light of their limited resources.

VI

FOREIGN RELATIONS—"THE WESTERN QUESTION"

It can be argued that the slow reversal of Ottoman imperial fortunes and the attainment of European superiority which constituted the nineteenth-century "Eastern Question" had an exact parallel in Algerine-European relations in the western Mediterranean during the same period. This "Western Question" was not of course limited to Algiers; it concerned in varying degrees Sherifian Morocco, Beylical Tunis, and the Pashalik of Tripoli as well. But Algiers was pivotal. It could not be legislated out of existence or absorbed into some larger territorial unit. Nor could it be reattached directly to the Ottoman dominions (as was the case with Tripoli) in order to forestall European acquisition. The Ottoman forces by that time lacked the power, even if they had wished to do so, to invade Algiers.

What proved to be the Achilles heel of the Regency, the obligations of the French government to the Jewish financiers Busnach and Bacri, came about through an unfortunate combination of circumstances and personalities. Otherwise, for three centuries Algerine foreign relations were conducted in such a manner as to preserve and advance the state's interests in total indifference to the actions of its adversaries, and to enhance Ottoman interests in the process. Algerine foreign policy was flexible, imaginative, and subtle; it blended an absolute conviction of naval superiority and belief in the permanence of the state as a vital cog in the political community of Islam, with a profound understanding of the fears, ambitions, and rivalries of Christian Europe.

Algerine self-assurance and the Algerine belief in the inviolability of its territory were well founded in view of the constant failure of European expeditions sent against the Regency. Except for Oran, whose possession was contested intermittently by the Spanish and the Turks until the final cession to Algiers in 1792, and the coral-fishery factory (the Bastion) granted to the Compagnie Lenche, no portion of the Regency passed into foreign hands until the French conquest.

The external relations of Algiers fell into three broad categories: those with neighboring Maghrib states, Algerine-European relations, and relations with the Ottoman Porte. In the first and second cases, the basic Algerine objective was the same, namely, to avert the formation of any combination or bloc powerful enough to dislodge the Regency or threaten internal security. However, the nature of the North African coastline and the religious affinity precluded Algerine operations against other Muslim corsairs.

Campaigns such as those undertaken against Tunis by Algerine land forces were intended to secure compliance by Tunisian rulers with the hegemony of Algiers, within the over-all framework of indirect Ottoman rule in North Africa. After the recovery of Tunis for the Ottomans by Uluç Ali and Sinan Pasha in 1574, the Tunisian Regency was established on the Algerine model, with a pasha appointed by the Porte and advised by a divan of senior officers of the *ocak* plus Tunis notables. Subsequently, in 1591 the *ocak* rebelled and established one of its own officers as second in command to the pasha, but responsible for law and order. After various vicissitudes, government in Tunisia was finally vested in a line of beys in a form of dynastic rule which generated periodic friction between the two regencies as the deys of Algiers sought to intervene in various Tunisian dynastic quarrels.

The most serious of these quarrels occurred in the eighteenth century. Dey Haci Mustafa, acting upon the assassination of the last Muradid bey, Ali, marched to Tunis in 1705, seized the city, and took the principal conspirator in the assassination, the agha of the spahis, back with him to Algiers as a prisoner. The founder of the Husseinids, Hussein ibn Ali, came to power as the result of organizing the Tunisian resistance to the Algerine invasion.

Algiers intervened in Tunisian affairs again after the death of Hussin ibn Ali in 1740, supporting his sons against the claim of his nephew to the beylical throne. The invasion was beaten off in 1756, and thereafter the beys devoted their efforts to building up a prosperous commerce and a disciplined army of Turks as well as irregular spahi cavalry to resist further Algerine incursions. A complicating factor arose from the fact that the bey of Constantine at the time cherished ambitions of enlarging his beylik at Tunisian expense. After leading an occupation army to Tunis, he attempted to persuade Baba Ali (*Parmaksiz*) Dey either to annex the state or at least to impose tribute on the reinstated sons of Hussein ibn Ali. But the dey refused, on the grounds that to do so would violate the obligations which both regencies held toward the Ottoman sultan.

A second series of Algero-Tunisian conflicts occurred during the Napoleonic period. Although refraining from the collection of tribute, the Algerine deys had exacted as the price of their support of the Husseinids the right to sell their livestock in Tunis at fixed prices ahead of the Tunisian livestock, to commandeer the official beylical guesthouse at the Bardo for their emissaries, and to receive from Tunis supplies of olive oil sufficient to maintain the mosques of Algiers. Hammuda Bey (1777–1813) gave notice of his intent in 1806 to defy these commitments. He granted asylum to the deposed bey of Constantine, Mustafa (whose mother was an Englishwoman, hence his surname Ingiliz), and refused to authorize the sale of Algerine livestock in Tunis at higher than market prices. A Tunisian army then invaded Algeria, but was driven back. The Algerines returned the favor, but were defeated on three occasions, including an attempt to seize Tunis by sea. Peace was then re-established between the two regencies. However, ill feeling seems to have persisted, giving in the end an ironic twist in that the bey's refusal to impede the French conquest of Algiers—Tunisian authorities not only co-operated with French forces but prevented an

Ottoman envoy from landing—resulted in the eventual absorption by France of both regencies.

Relations between Algiers and the Sherifian Empire of Morocco were strongly competitive during the early period of the Regency, but less so there after. Rivalry in the sixteenth century revolved around control of Tlemcen (Tilimsan) and the surrounding region. The Ziyanid rulers of Tlemcen attempted to remain independent of both the Spaniards and the Turks, allying themselves with whichever side seemed to have the upper hand. By 1545 Spain held only a precarious foothold in Oran. At this point the Saadians, sherifs from southern Morocco who ruled in Marrakesh, moved northward and seized the northern Moroccan capital of Fez. The Tlemcenis, whose traditional cultural and religious ties were with Fez, invited the Saadians to occupy the city. This brought on a conflict which ended with their expulsion by the Turks; henceforth except for Oran the whole of western Algeria was incorporated into the Regency.

Algerine intervention in Moroccan affairs reached a peak in the latter part of the seventeenth century with the accession of the Alawite sherifs to the Moroccan throne. Moulay Ismail pursued the "Holy War" with the Turks with vigor, but Saban Dey, with a force of six thousand Janissaries and four thousand cavalry, routed the Sherifian force of some seventy thousand. Algerines backed the north Moroccan tribal leader Ghailan against Moulay Ismail in a revolt intended to replace the sultan with his nephew. Ghailan was defeated and killed in 1673, and thereafter the Turks shifted their attention elsewhere, while Morocco entered a period of isolation which lasted until the late nineteenth century.

Algerine-European relations were infinitely more complex. The international legal question posed by the adherence of the Regency of the Porte, although it was the subject of considerable correspondence, did not deter Algiers from pursuing an independent foreign policy. European representation in Algiers was maintained by consuls, the first accredited European representative being the consul of France. A. M. Bartholle, of Marseille, was nominated in 1564 but subsequently, the intervention of François de Noailles, Bishop of Dax, with the sultan secured the appointment of Maurice Sauron as the first French consul in 1578.

Algerine strategy toward Europe was to prevent any combination of European adversaries powerful enough to converge on the well-guarded city and overthrow the *ocak*. The strategy was pursued in various forms—through regular demands for tribute, preferential treatment in prisoner release arrangements according to nationality, selectivity in corsair targets, and formal peace treaties. Algiers also subscribed to certain of the treaty commitments of the Porte and was mentioned in corresponding fashion. Similarly the correspondence of the various deys with France, as an example, confirmed the adherence of Algiers to the Ottoman sultan.

As one might expect from a power which had originated as a maritime city-state, the implementation of a successful foreign policy rested ultimately with the Algerine corsair fleet. Yet it is a curious fact that this fleet in size, armaments, and effectiveness varied considerably during the period of existence of the Regency, and at various times was virtually written off by its opponents as a serious threat to Mediterranean commerce or political stability. Inasmuch as the Ottoman government not only furnished no naval assistance to Algiers but also requisitioned on occasion (Lepanto being an example) Algerine naval support, the ability of Algiers to rebound from naval adversity was quite remarkable.

In 1530, the fleet assembled at Algiers by Kheireddin was said to number sixty wooden ships. Kheireddin's departure for Constantinople must have reduced the effectives available to his successor on land as well as on sea, for we are told that Hassan Beylerbey could muster against the Spanish fleet of 65 galleys and 460 transports carrying 37,000 soldiers and marines only the garrison of six hundred Turks and a few thousand Arab auxiliaries. The successful repulse of the expedition gave new life to the naval power of Algiers. By 1571 the Algerine fleet consisted of fifty galleys, galliots, and brigantines. Haedo counted thirty-six galleys in 1581, each with between fifteen and twenty-four benches of oars (eight oarsmen per bench), plus thirty brigantines; each bench had a complement of four Janissaries assigned to it.

These sixteenth-century corsair ships utilized human brawn, Janissary ferocity, and the powerful ram's beak fitted into the ships' bows to achieve tactical superiority over the European enemies. The perfection of naval gunnery in the seventeenth century and the development of large, far-heavier-armed sailing ships produced a corresponding change in the composition of the Algerine fleet. There being no lack of renegade recruits for the ranks of the *taife*, the skills brought to Algiers by European artificers enabled the fleet to maintain its effectiveness, although individual vessels and corsair squadrons found themselves frequently outnumbered if not outgunned.

In the early seventeenth century the composition of the *taife* underwent a significant change, occasioned by the relative parity between European and Ottoman naval strength, which evolved after Lepanto, and the active intrusion of northern European powers into Mediterranean affairs. Algiers benefited in several ways. The widening of European rivalries and their transfer to the Mediterranean brought vastly increased opportunities to the *ocak* to apply its traditional *divide et impera* tactics toward its adversaries. In theory such powers as France, England, and probably Holland represented greater individual threats to Algerine sovereignty than the city-states or princedoms of the Mediterranean basin. But in fact collusion in the matter of naval expeditions proved to be nearly impossible. Friendship with Algiers rather than chastisement was the rule, however much its naval depradations angered European rulers, because such friendship could be used to advantage by England against France, France against Spain, and so on.

Equally important to Algerine foreign policy was the general shift in naval warfare and tactics with the development of the sailing ship of the line, with its tremendous firepower and speed and its ability to navigate oceanic waters. English, Dutch, and Flemish renegades, men already familiar with such vessels, introduced them to Algiers. One of the most valuable in terms of his contributions to his adopted country was Simon Danser (or Dansa), a Dutchman from Dordrecht. Danser came to Algiers from Marseille, where he had established residence, married, and engaged in the shipbuilding trade. It is not clear what caused him to turn renegade and understake a corsair career, but within three years of his arrival he had become the *taife's* leading reis and had acquired the surname of Deli-Reis, "Captain Devil," for his audacious exploits. Using captured prizes as models, Danser taught his fellow captains the management and navigation of round ships, equipped with high decks, banks of sails, and cannon. He personally accounted for forty prizes, which were incorporated into the corsair fleet, and from Danser's time onward the Algerines replenished their losses equally from captured ships and from their own shipyard.

Danser also led the Algerines farther afield than they had ever navigated before. They passed through the Strait of Gibraltar, penetrated the Atlantic, and ranged as far north as Iceland, where a corsair squadron swept the coast in 1616. Other *reisi* ranged the Bay of Biscay in cooperation with the Moroccan corsairs of Salé, who provided them with anchorage and provisions on request, even during Moulay Ismail's wars with the Regency. In 1623–24 Algerine corsairs sacked Iskenderun (Alexandretta), apparently to protest restrictions on their activities in the eastern Mediterranean by the Porte, and in 1637 they entered the English Channel to raid along the French coast.

Ironically, Danser, who seems to have retained his Christian faith at least in secret, utilized the capture of a Spanish ship carrying ten Jesuit priests off Valencia as a means of informing the French Court of Henri IV secretly of his intention to return to Marseille, where he had left his wife and children. The French agreed on condition of the safe return of the Jesuits, which was done. In 1609 Danser was reunited with his family and restored to full citizenship by the Marseille city council. But, once a corsair always a corsair, whether in the service of Christian France or Muslim Algiers, and in 1610 Danser presented to the king and the Marseille councilors a bold proposal for an expedition against Algiers which—given his extraordinary inside knowledge of the city—would probably have overthrown the Regency government. Unfortunately, the French, distrustful of the loyalty of the former corsair, refused to entertain his project.

Aside from manpower, Algiers reaped a continuing harvest of ships and prisoners from its naval campaigns. In most cases captured ships were towed into port, repaired, refitted, and returned to sea with new names under appointed corsair captains. In 1619, for example, the fleet consisted of three oared galleys and seventy-two sail-powered ships of war, as compared with thirty-five galleys in 1588. In 1623 Algiers had seventy-five ships of the line and a hundred miscellaneous vessels. In 1659 the fleet consisted of twenty-three sailing galleys, each with fifty guns and a complement of four-hundred crewmen. By the early eighteenth century half of the fleet had been built elsewhere, a fact which simplified the task of the Algerine marine arsenal in maintaining Regency naval strength at parity with that of Europe. The losses caused by the various European naval expeditions launched against Algiers ,probably because they were not followed up by land operations or enforceable peace treaties, failed to curtail seriously Algerine naval operations right through the Napoleonic Wars and into the post-Napoleonic period.

The last great corsair captain, Reis Hamida, played a key role in the preservation of Algiers through these critical times. In 1802, he captured a forty-four-gun Portuguese frigate without the loss of a man. The vessel, rechristened *Portekiza* swept the Mediterranean under his leadership and in 1809 passed the Strait of Gibraltar with two other frigates. Had Hamida not been surprised, alone, in 1815 by Stephen Decatur's squadron off Cape de Gata and killed in the running gun fight which followed, it seems likely that the revival of Algerine fortunes generated by his seamanship would have continued for a much longer period. Even so, the Algerines were able to restore the losses (including the destruction of *Portekiza* in Algiers harbor in 1816) caused by Exmouth without difficulty. As late as 1825 their fleet had four frigates totaling 188 guns, plus two corvettes and two brigs, with a total firepower which could hold its own in any company.

The question of corsair captives dominated Algiers' relations with Europe. Between 1621 and 1627 there were said to be twenty thousand Christian captives in the corsair capital, including "Portuguese, Flemish, Scots, English, Danes, Irish, Hungarians, Slavs, Spanish, French, Italian; also Syrians, Egyptians, Japanese, Chinese, South Americans, Ethiopians," which attests to the polygot ethnicity of seafaring in those days. The records kept by Redemptionists on apostasy are equally revealing, although painful to the apostolic ego. Between 1609 and 1619, Gramaye observed, renegades who willingly abjured their faith for the comforts of Islam included "857 Germans, 138 Hamburgmen, 300 English, 130 Dutch and Flemings, 160 Danes and Easterlings, 250 Poles, Hungarians and Muscovites."

The continued depradations of the corsairs produced some unexpected friction between the Algerines and the Porte when the latter began to engage in treaty relations with Europe in recognition of the growing parity of forces in the Mediterranean. Several treaties between the Porte and Christian powers contained references to this problem. The Ottoman treaty of July 6, 1612, with Holland, entitled "Capitulations and Privileges Accorded by Sultan Ahmet I to the United Provinces of the Low Countries," noted in Article XXI:

As to the Corsairs of Algiers and Barbary entering the ports of the Low Countries, as it is customary to show them courtesy and provide them with powder lead, even sails, all that they need; so it is not my wish that when they shall encounter ships of the Low Countries they seize their merchandise and lead them captives but they shall release all captives and restore to them their effects, and if the Corsairs . . . of Algiers and Barbary disobey my orders they shall not be received peaceably in your ports. . . .

These stipulations and provisions were renewed in the Treaty of Commerce of 1680 signed by the Dutch with Mehmed IV. The Ottoman-Venetian Treaty of Passarowitz (July 21, 1718), the treaty of commerce of 1756 with Denmark, and the treaty of April 7, 1740, between the Porte and Charles II, King of the Two Sicilies, contained similar language in implicit recognition that the corsairs were bound by the same international codes of behavior as those that linked Ottomans and Europeans in a family of nations. The 1737 treaty between Sweden and the Porte required the sultan to ensure compliance of the three regencies with an earlier peace treaty which the Swedes had signed in 1729 with Algiers, Tunis, and Tripoli. In 1739 Mahmud I inserted into the renewal agreement with Sweden a clause (Article VIII) to the effect that all the foreign relations of the North African states required concurrence by the Porte, inasmuch as they were sovereign Ottoman territory.

In reality these restrictions on Algerine freedom of action were more moral than pragmatic. Thus the suppression of the Janissary order by Mahmud II in 1826 was not followed by a corresponding dissolution of the *ocak* in Algiers. Militarism and militant Islam governed its foreign relations—Algiers would not legitimately initiate treaties with foreign Christian nations, or bind itself to keep the terms of an armistice, without violating the principles on which the state had been founded. Herein lies the outstanding difference between the Ottoman Porte and its remote dependency. With rare exceptions the deys, pushed into office by fractious compatriots and subject to sudden replacement, pursued Algerine foreign policy based on belief in the superiority of the state over its opponents, demanded gifts and/or tribute as their just due, and avoided the trap of military defeat followed by territorial concessions and religious protectionism which brought growing direct intervention on the part of Russia, Britain, and other European states in internal Ottoman affairs.

Tribute was the key to Algerine-European relations. Europe paid tribute because it could not or would not develop a consistent policy of collective action against Algiers. Tribute was individually protective; it was also advantageous to small European powers who relied on peaceful commerce for survival. The Algerines in turn, though they might increase their tribute levies from year to year on individual countries or demand richer presents from resident European consuls, were generally scrupulous in abstaining from attacks on the ships or ports of tribute-paying nations. The same arrangement applied to European ports providing services to corsair vessels. The Italian port of Livorno (Leghorn), for example, consistently granted them harborage and refitting facilities, and as a result was never visited with fire and sword as were its neighbors.

Marseille enjoyed a similar exemption. Until 1718 the French consuls resident at Algiers were paid by the Marseille

Chamber of Commerce. The Chamber was also the sole French agency permitted by the deys to issue residence permits for French nationals in Algiers who were not diplomatic representatives. The instance described by Nicolay in 1551 of "a ship of Marseille there in Bona, conducted by a corsair, to gather coral" was a continuation of a practice which actually predates the establishment of the Regency. As early as the twelfth century the municipality of Marseille signed a treaty with the sultan of Bougie granting the Marseillais the right to station a consul there and for their ships to trade without hindrance.

Presents were also brought to the deys by new consuls arriving to take up residence in Algiers. The Venetian consul in 1778, for example, presented gifts equal in value to thirty thousand gold ducats. The commander of the Venetian escort squadron, Angelo Emo, a nobleman, was allowed as a mark of honor to accompany the consul and to be seated in the presence of the dey in return for a present equal in value to that presented by the consul and in recognition of his social status—and Emo paid! Earlier, the grand duke of Tuscany had signified his acceptance of the friendship treaty of 1718 with Algiers with the gift of a diamond-studded trunk. In 1816 France, England, Spain, and Holland each paid tribute totaling 580,000 piasters (about $696,000) and Sweden and Denmark made tribute payments of $254,000, for a total of $950,000 in extra legal revenue.

Tributary payments, although they represented a periodic drain on European exchequers, preserved the trading balance in the Mediterranean and permitted lesser nations such as Denmark and Holland to maintain the favorable balance necessary to their economies. The comment of a

Genoese merchant, "to trade in Algiers ensures 30% profit," is indicative of the general pattern. When Bossuet, giving the oration at the obsequies of Maria Theresa, declaimed, "You are wont to say, Algiers, 'I hold the sea under my laws; all nations are my lawful prey; the swiftness of my ships gives me confidence'," he was not so much being rhetorical as stating a fact of Mediterranean commercial life.

The various European expeditions undertaken against Algiers demonstrate graphically the ineptness of European foreign policy (in the collective sense) when confronted with a determined, united, and internally strong nation. The disastrous attempt of Charles V in 1541 was described in Chapter I. Some years later one Juan Gascon, a native of Valencia, conceived a plan not disimilar from Decatur's two centuries later, and obtained approval from Philip II to sail secretly to Algiers and blow up the entire corsair fleet in harbor, choosing the autumn equinoctial season for his expedition because the corsairs usually were laid up for refitting at that time. Gascon set sail early in October and reached Algiers without interference. With great boldness he touched anchor at the end of the mole built by Kheireddin, leaving his dagger stuck in the outer door as proof of his courage. But the clumsiness of his men in preparing their muskets alarmed the sleeping garrison, and Gascon was forced to set sail before he could carry out his plan. Several Algerine galliots gave chase, and one of them captured him.

Gascon was sentenced to death by impalement, the sentence being promptly executed. Before the bold Spaniard had expired, however, several corsair captains made representations to the reigning pasha, to the effect that prisoners of war deserved a better fate, especially as Gascon had contrived the same sort of conspiracy against Algiers as they themselves were wont to practice against nations at war with them. They warned the pasha that such treatment might provoke the Spanish to similar reprisals against Algerine captains. As a result, Gascon was taken down from his hook and his wounds attended by some Christian doctors. Unfortunately, the action aroused the fury of the populace, notably the Moriscos lately arrived from Spain, and the exasperated pasha once more ordered Gascon dropped from the city wall onto his hook, this time to expire for good.

Subsequent naval expeditions against Algiers produced equally meager results. The Spanish bombarded the city in 1601, the French in 1617, the English for the first time in 1620 under Sir Robert Mansell. (The first English treaty with Algiers, signed in 1682, was largely due to the efforts of Consul Samuel Martin (1674–80), who promised the Divan in 1676 that England would limit the number of foreigners traveling aboard her vessels and would not provoke attacks on Algerine corsairs, if in return English commercial ships would not be molested or be required to submit to the pass system or search by the corsairs.) In 1670 an English squadron commanded by Sir Thomas Allen captured and burned six corsair brigantines totaling 248 guns off Cape Spartel, but did not follow up his success. In 1770 the Danes, led by the admiral Count de Kaas, bombarded Algiers from a distance but found themselves too far offshore to sustain their bombardment; they then withdrew and resumed tribute payments in 1772.

The second serious attempt on the part of Spain to seize the citadel of her ancient enemy took place in 1775. As was the case with the "grand crusade" of Charles V, the Spaniards were fired with zeal for the destruction of the headquarters of anti-Christendom. On June 23, 1775, an armada of 51 warships and 170 troop transports under the command of Admiral Don Pedro de Castijon set sail from Algeciras. A week later it anchored in the Bay of Algiers. The troop transports carried 24,447 men, mostly Spanish, but included complements of Swiss and Walloon guardsmen; their commander was an Irish soldier of fortune, "General" Alexander O'Reilly. Against this Spanish power Dey Baba Mohammed could muster but three thousand members of the *ocak*. Ibrahim, the bey of Oran, responded to his appeal for jihad with four thousand spahis, and later on Salah, the bey of Constantine, would arrive with twenty thousand. But the key to defense of Algiers as always was its forts and guns, and its famous mystique which had overawed so many visitors over the years. The insouciant Algerines were not at all impressed by the spectacle of the huge Spanish fleet, moored just beyond cannon range, each vessel flying every standard and banner it could lay its hands on. "Just another *espagnolade*" (the word used by the corsairs to describe any enterprise whose end failed to correspond with its grandeur, pomp, or preparations), scoffed the dey.

And so it happened. After a lengthy delay, the Spanish detached one of their warships, the *San-Josef*, and sent it to destroy the most exposed of the Algerine shore batteries. The attempt was successful, and on July 8, a Spanish detachment of 12,000 men, half the available force, was disembarked on the left bank of the Harrach not far from the spot where Charles V's marines had landed. The omens seemed more favorable this time, as a clear morning dawned under a brilliant African sun. The Spaniards finding no opposition—

133

the Algerines were not expecting a land operation—began to march toward the city, some twelve miles to the west.

Meanwhile, the armada ranged itself along the coast so as to cover the infantrymen with protective fire once the force met opposition. Unfortunately, O'Reilly seems to have neglected the most elemental precautions of armies in unknown, hostile country, establishing no redoubts in case of retreat, and keeping his forces close together without use of scouts. He also failed to capture an insignificant gun battery, held by a scant dozen men, which guarded the Harrach estuary. Its capture would have enabled him to maintain the element of surprise established by the landing. The Turks turned the guns around after the Spanish had passed by and poured a withering fire on the invaders from the rear. The spahis of the bey of Constantine harrassed the Spanish with the swift charges which Emir Abdelkader would use to similar effect against the French in his campaigns of 1834–47. In addition, a troop of Arab cameleers distracted the Spanish infantrymen, more by the mere presence of the camels than by any military advantage they represented, since the bey lost sixty or seventy of them to enemy musket fire.

A more serious mistake affected a line of march close to the beach, for, although this route avoided the heavy maquis undergrowth which inland would have delayed them and subjected them to intermittent ambushes, it brought them under the fire of their own ships. After several hours of struggle, the invasion force fought its way back to the water's edge, a few miles from its original landing point, and what was left of it reembarked in the waiting longboats. Major William Dalrymple, an English officer who accompanied the expedition, wrote in a letter from Gibraltar on October 1,

1775, "Spanish losses were 27 officers killed, 191 wounded, 501 men killed, 2088 wounded," adding, "the Moors [*sic*] did not leave a wounded Spaniard alive, for the Government of Algiers had offered a premium of 10 sequins for each Spanish head."

O'Reilly's expedition was the last European attempt at a combined land and sea invasion of Algiers, but it was only the penultimate Spanish attempt. In 1783 the stubborn Spanish tried again, with a fleet of thirty-one vessels under the command of Don Antonio Barcelo. The fleet was delayed twenty-seven days at sea after its departure from Cartagena on July 2, because of unfavorable winds and the inconvenience caused by the presence of so many small vessels and the transport of heavy artillery. The blessings invoked by Barcelo from heaven upon Christian arms by formal departure ceremonies were as ineffective on this occasion as in the previous Spanish expeditions. The battle between Spanish guns and Algerine shore batteries was joined on August 1 and continued for nine days without letup, with a total expenditure of 3,723 bombs and 3,853 cannon shot against Algiers and return fire from the shore batteries of 399 bombs and 11,284 cannon shot. This vast unloading of fire produced no permanent damage on either side; the Algerines put out their fires almost as quickly as they were ignited, while the Spanish superiority of fire precluded any successful attacks by Algerine vessels on the Spanish battle line.

With the decline of Spanish power in the Mediterranean and of Spain's interest in North Africa, Algerine foreign relations during the final period of the Regency's existence achieved a certain equilibrium between British and French interests. The emergence of the United States as an independent nation introduced a new element, one which the Algerienes sought to exploit quickly in pursuit of their traditional policy toward Europe of "divide and prosper," as well as an added source of tribute, inasmuch as treaties with England, France, Sardinia, and Holland exempted those nations from payment of tribute. The dey, insisting on the customary rights of search and seizure in the absence of any treaty agreement with a new nation, declared war, and in 1785 Algerine corsairs cruising beyond the Strait of Gibraltar seized two American vessels in the Atlantic not far from the port of Salé.

The two actions had the effect of excluding American trade from the Mediterranean, but, because of a state of war between Algiers and Portugal, a Portuguese naval force was stationed in the strait of sufficient size to deter the passage of corsair squadrons in strength, and the United States trade was not seriously affected until 1793. In that year the English negotiated a peace treaty between Algiers and Portugal, and as a consequence the corsairs were in effect released from their Mediterranean confinement. They promptly swept the Spanish and northern Moroccan coasts and the Bay of Biscay, bringing in eleven American ships as prizes to Algiers, with more than a hundred captive American sailors.

Colonel David Humphreys, United States minister to Portugal, was appointed by President Adams to negotiate a peace treaty with Algiers which would secure the release of the prisoners. Humphreys designated Joseph Donaldson to go to Algiers to conduct the negotiations, which he did, and in September, 1795, a peace treaty was obtained with the Regency which bound the United States to pay $642,500 for the ransom of the 101 surviving prisoners and as presents to the Algerine government. Dey Hassan on his part agreed to intervene with the other two Regencies to secure peace treaties on behalf of the American government. The treaty was ratified by the Senate on March 2, 1796; it bound the United States to an annual tribute of 12,000 Algerine sequins ($21,600) in naval stores in addition to the ransom commitment made by Donaldson and paid by his successor Joel Barlow, United States interim commissioner to Algiers, the delay being caused by the parlous state of American finances which made it very difficult to raise the necessary sum.

The treaty placed the United States in the same position as other smaller European nations in relation to the Regency, albeit with the advantages of less vulnerability due to distance and a reduced tribute. American warships would be given the standard twenty gun salute on arrival in Algiers harbor. The United States was to be represented by a resident consul, whose diplomatic status was confirmed and for whom a dwelling was rented from the heirs of Dey Mustafa (1798–1805).

In consequence of the treaty, Algerine-American relations remained peaceful during the period of European upheavals which produced the Napoleonic Wars, with United States Consul General Tobias Lear and after him Consul William Shaler providing a moderating influence on the deys which earned the United States much good will in Algiers. American ships delivered the annual tribute in naval stores on schedule. However, a certain European resentment over the emergence of America as a trading rival, combined with the intrigues of the French and British consuls in Algiers and

the recurrence of instability within the Algerine government (signaled by the executions of Baba Mustafa and Ali
Bursali), resulted in a renewal of hostilities.

Bursali's successor as dey, the agha of the *ocak*, Haci Ali,
declared war on the United States, in the same year, 1812,
alleging a violation of the 1795 treaty by the seizure of an
Algerine brig by Decatur's squadron. The ship was then
brought into Cartagena and there detained by the Spanish
government on grounds that it had been taken in Spanish
waters. The dey was apparently unware that the United
States was at war with Britain, with American naval strength
involved elsewhere and American commercial shipping giving the Mediterranean a wide berth. Except for the capture
of an American brig with a crew of eleven, Algiers derived no
benefit from the declaration. Shaler was compelled to leave
Algiers after the dey had refused to accept naval stores
brought by the *Allegheny* as tribute. The grounds were that
the quality of the powder was inferior. He returned in 1815
and negotiated a new treaty, which was renewed in 1816.

Aside from the general moral influence of the United
States consul on Algerine policies, England seems to have
exerted the greatest amount of positive moderation on the
Regency during the Napoleonic and post-Napoleonic periods,
although admittedly British self-interest more than altruism
dictated her actions. In 1810 the British secretary of legation
in Lisbon obtained a truce for Portugal with Algiers, which
gave the Portuguese a much-needed respite at sea while under
partial occupation and military assault by the French and
Spanish. The truce was converted into a treaty in 1812 by
William A'Court, British minister to the Barbary States, and,
though the cost to Portugal was heavy—$690,337 for the ran-

som of 615 Portuguese prisoners and $500,000 in additional tribute plus the usual presents—from then on Portuguese interests in Algiers came under British protection, with A'Court being named honorary consul of Portugal.

Similarly, in 1810 England sent a supply of naval and military stores to Algiers to compensate the Regency for the loss of tribute caused by the naval wars of European belligerents. In 1811 the British battleship *Undaunted* negotiated the release of the crew and cargo of a Spanish privateer (falsely accused of the sinking of a small Algerine coasting ship off Bona), with the payment of $70,000 in ransom money, through representations to the dey that the Spanish government could not raise any such sum, owing to wartime conditions.

Most interesting was a secret commitment on England's part, contained in a letter from the prince regent to the dey in 1812, by which "the Prince Regent in the name of his father George III . . . assures the Dey that he will protect his capital with his fleets, so long as the present friendship shall subsist between the two nations, . . . and begs the Dey not to permit those who are enemies of Great Britain to lessen the harmony now existing between the two nations." It seemed as if the two strongest naval powers in the Mediterranean had aligned their naval policies, with a defensive alliance on England's part declared as the sole condition of continuance of existing treaty obligations on the part of Algiers.

Four years later the English and the Algerines were at each others' throats, as Exmouth's cannon hammered the shore batteries of Algiers. The principal factor in this abrupt reversal of policy was the arrival of peace in Europe. With the withdrawal of French power from the territories along the Mediterranean controlled by Napoleon, the corsairs reasserted their boarding rights and resumed the taking of prizes, confident that this would produce a renewed flow of tribute. In July, 1814, seven Swedish ships were brought into Algiers and their cargoes, valued at five hundred thousand dollars, confiscated until the Swedish tribute ship arrived. In the following year Dey Ali, whose cruelty had become too much for the *ocak* and whose conduct of foreign affairs was suspect due to Decatur's success, was strangled in the hammam by seventy Janissaries. He was succeeded by Haci Mohammed, his *hazinedar*, an elderly man who at first refused the position, took it under protest, and for unknown reasons was himself strangled two weeks later and replaced by Omar, the agha of the *ocak*.

Omar's governance of the turbulent capital during his brief sojourn in office was characterized by firmness, energy, and considerable foresight. He wrote to the sultan reconfirming the ancient allegiance of Algiers, and to Moulay Abdullah of Morocco and Muhammad Ali, viceroy of Egypt, asking for their support against what he anticipated as a concerted European attack on Algiers. He reached peace agreements with the United States and with the kingdoms of Sardinia and Naples (in the latter two cases through English intervention). But events had moved beyond Omar's control. British subjects and the British consul in Algiers were manhandled and thrown into prison following the first visit of Exmouth (to obtain the above-mentioned agreements for Sardinia and Naples). Most serious of all was the event of May, 1816, at Bona, when two hundred coral fiishermen under British and French protection were surrounded and massacred while attending church. The Exmouth expedition of August, 1816, which followed brought disaster to Algiers.

The English fleet, bolstered with six Dutch frigates commanded by Admiral van Kappellen, moved into position under a flag of truce on the morning of August 27, 1816. The ultimatum to Algiers being refused, the *Queen Charlotte,* Exmouth's flagship (120 guns), stood away from the rest of the fleet and led the way into the inner harbor, anchoring within pistol shot of Kheireddin's mole. Other warships followed; then the British frigates took battle stations and the Dutch squadron moved into the line. Shaler was an eyewitness to the bombardment:

At exactly three o'clock a gun is fired by the Algerines upon the British admiral, and the battle instantly becomes general. At twenty minutes past three, the fire of the marine batteries appears to be silenced . . . at half past seven the shipping in the port is discovered to be on fire. At eight o'clock . . . the British Consul has been taken from his house by an armed band and is confined in heavy chains in the common prison. . . . At nine, the fire begins to slacken on both sides. . . . At midnight everything in the port appears to be in flames. . . . A black thunderstorm is rising; its vivid lightning discovers the hostile fleets retiring with the land breeze. . . . The morning of the twenty-eighth discovers that the Algerines are unable to make any further resistance. . . . In the course of the day [they] acknowledge themselves vanquished. . . . Algiers has suffered a prodigious loss in shipping and . . . all her defensive works.

The tenth "Battle of Algiers" was costly to both sides

despite the thoroughness of the British victory. On the Algerine side Exmouth reported losses as follows:

Memorandum of the Destruction in the Mole of Algiers, in the Attack of the 27th August, 1816

Four large frigates of forty-four guns; five large corvettes from twenty-four to thirty; all the gun and mortar boats except seven, thirty destroyed; several merchant brigs and schooners; a great number of small vessels of various descriptions; all the pontoons, lighters, &c., storehouses, and arsenal, with all the timber and various marine articles, destroyed in part; a great many gun-carriages, mortar-beds, casks, and ships' stores of all descriptions.

But casualties were heavy among the invasion fleet as well. The *Impregnable* alone sustained a loss of 150 killed and wounded, while a rocket boat with two officers and nine crew blew up in the firing of one of the Algerine frigates. When it was over the dey accepted the original peace conditions brought to Algiers under the flag of truce. There were five conditions: the abolition of the practice of imprisonment of Christian prisoners; the surrender of all prisoners in the Regency; the return of ransom payments received during the year; compensation to the British consul for his confinement; and a public apology made to the consul upon his release by the dey. The change of fortunes experienced by the Regency in its relations with Europe is vividly illustrated by Exmouth's second memorandum, sent on August 28, to the dey:

His Britannic Majesty's ship Queen Charlotte,
Algiers Bay, August 28th, 1816

Sir,

For your atrocities at Bona, on defenceless Christians, and your unbecoming disregard of the demands I made yesterday, in the name of the Prince Regent of England, the fleet under my orders has given you a signal chastisement, by the total destruction of your navy, storehouses, and arsenal, with half your batteries.

As England does not war for the destruction of cities, I am unwilling to visit your personal cruelties upon the inoffensive inhabitants of the country, and therefore offer you the same terms of peace which I conveyed to you yesterday in my sovereign's name; without the acceptance of these terms, you can have no peace with England.

If you receive this offer as you ought, you will fire three guns; and I shall consider your not making this signal as a refusal, and shall renew my operations at my own convenience.

I offer you the above terms, provided neither the British Consul, nor the officers and men so wickedly seized by you from the boats of a British ship of war, have met with any cruel treatment, or any of the Christian slaves in your power; and repeat my demand, that the Consul and officers and men, may be sent off to me, conformably to ancient treaties. I have, E&c

[Signed] Exmouth

The Sardinian and Neapolitan ransom monies were returned, and all prisoners released, and Omar bound himself to observe the peaceful conduct of naval affairs defined in the Congress of Vienna and the Peace of Paris. As Prince Regent William (later William IV) told a delegation of

London citizens who waited on him, "The treaty of peace was such as a great and generous nation should accord its enemies."

Yet in the long run the expedition accomplished little more than its nine predecessors in defining a viable Mediterranean relationship between Algiers and its transmaritime neighbors. Ironically, although the English battle plan called for punishment rather than occupation, the state of Algiers' defenses after the bombardment was such that a detachment of Royal marines could have taken the city with ease, and the Regency would then have come under British control, with vastly different consequences for the future of North Africa.

The resilience of Algiers on this occasion was characteristic. Following the defeat, Dey Omar devoted extraordinary efforts to the rebuilding of Algiers' defenses and the restoration of its links with the Ottoman Empire, reaffirming Algerine allegiance to the sultan in his request for three frigates to be sent him from the Constantinople shipyard. His efforts restored Algiers to its normal state of readiness. But the ignominy of the defeat required a sacrifice; face had been lost by the public apology to the British consul. In January, 1817, the soldiers surrounded his palace. Omar offered double pay to all members of the *ocak* if they spared him, but the offer was rejected. The Janissaries seized and bound him; he was then strangled at the place of public execution, after which the soldiers returned to their barracks. The whole procedure required less than an hour!

It now remains to consider the relationship of Algiers to the Ottoman Porte. It was Ottoman practice from the Treaty of Carlowitz (1683) onward to include reference to the corsair states in all instruments signed with Christian powers. In this fashion the sultans justified their commitment to the jihad by identification of the corsairs as their instrument of sacred action.

The *Sened*, or obligatory instrument, issued by Abdul Hamid I for the Austrian Court is a good example of this policy. In this document, issued the ninth of Ramadan 1197 (August 8, 1783) and forwarded under vizierial cachet to the Austrian ambassador, Abdul Hamid bound himself to require as far as possible the corsairs "coming from the provinces of Barbary," to observe the existing peace between the two empires, and in the event of violations to compel the corsairs to make restitution of captives and prizes taken among vessels flying the Austrian flag and furnished with imperial passports (including those from German ports) and of damages where sustained. The sultan also bound himself to furnish indemnification from Ottoman resources in the event "complete satisfaction is not obtained from the corsairs within a period of six months of demand," and to permit "reprisals against these Ottoman borderlands if necessary in order to obtain satisfactory reclamation of property and prisoners." A firman addressed to the three regencies in February, 1814, ordered them to comply with the earlier commitments, which in the language of the document applied not only to the high seas but also to ships forced into North African ports by weather or other difficulties.

On their part, the Algerines went to considerable lengths on various occasions to emphasize their loyalty to the empire as the heartland of Islam. None of their sovereigns, whether beylerbey, pasha, or dey, were clothed with attributes higher than those of the ordinary temporal ruler. The minting of coinage, Friday *khotbas* (sermons) and prayers in the

mosques were in the sultan's name and were offered for his
health and prosperity as caliph. The vesting of authority in a
resident dey in the early eighteenth century represented a
recognition of practical facts rather than a transfer of authority; the practice of a firman of investiture continued, as did
the references in Algerine diplomatic correspondence to the
Regency's status within the empire. Writing to the comte
de Pontchartrain in 1706, Dey Hussein begins his letter,
". . . from the powerful Hussein Effendi, Șerif of the family
of Hussein, by the grace and help of God Dey and Com-
mander-in-Chief of the powerful city of Algiers in Africa,
subject of the mighty Emperor of the Ottomans." Dey Ali,
writing to Louis XIV in 1711, is even more effusive, referring
to "Algiers, one of the kingdoms under the jurisdiction of
the majestic Sultan Ahmed, heir to the House of Osman, by
the grace of God ruler of all Muslims, whose Caliphate God
shall preserve and perpetuate until the Day of Judgment. . . ."

The interdependence of empire and regency is perhaps
best illustrated by the support each gave the other in times
of crisis. Apart from the Ottoman role in legitimizing the
conquests of Aruj and Kheireddin, Algiers furnished naval
units at Lepanto and on other occasions. Algerine ships took
an active part in the efforts of the Ottoman fleet to drive
Napoleon from Egypt, and detachments from the *ocak* helped
to curb rebellions against the Porte's authority by the Mam-
luks and in the Lebanon; an Algerine *yoldaş* killed Bashir
III, the last governor of Acre before Djezzar Pasha. Because
the corsairs were in essence a component of the Ottoman
navy, their captains could be deputized on demand for higher
service and individuals recompensed for some signal or heroic
contribution to the cause of Islam out of the imperial treasury.

The bulk of correspondence between the Porte and Algiers preserved in the Ottoman archives concerned actions of this nature. The *Hŭkŭm* (Command) addressed to Dey Hŭseyin Mezamorta in 1683, after his inspirational leadership had salvaged Algiers from defeat at the hands of Duquesne's French squadrons, advised Hŭseyin,

I had planned to use your services in a higher state capacity, but because of the requests of your people and your great capabilities in naval science I have decided to keep you at your present position. However I shall require your assistance as commander of the naval squadrons of the province in the great campaign against the unbelievers [notably those of Venice] who have harmed the islands and coasts of Islam. . . . This is my wish and firman *and hence irrevocable.*

Mezamorta's later appointment as *Kapudan derya*, apparently the higher state position referred to, was a consequence of these contributions. Not only the Algerine heads of state, but corsair captains themselves, had no hesitation in addressing the sultan directly with requests for a bonus, promotion, or similar mark of favor, for individuals whose bravery in land or sea campaigns merited some recognition by the head of Islam.

VII

THE FRENCH CONQUEST

The end of the corsair state was accomplished in the same abrupt, unexpected fashion as its beginning, only in reverse. A hesitant French expeditionary force, from its landfall on the opposite side of Algiers from the landing site of Charles V's infantry, moved through rough maquis terrain against harassing but disorganized opposition in June and July, 1830, until they reached the city's western gates. The ancient superstition that one day soldiers in scarlet cloaks would overcome Algiers from the land side was fulfilled in a sort of classical Greek scenario. The penultimate scene had been played earlier, as a proud Turk tapped an equally proud Frenchman on the shoulder with a fly whisk. From this incident events moved to their logical conclusion. As the French forces marched into the corsair capital they were greeted with silence, although the shops of Algerine merchants remained open and grave men sitting at cafes continued to sip Turkish coffee and smoke their water pipes. It was as if an age had ended and no one cared.

Behind the capitulation of Hussein, the last dey of Algiers, and the absorption of the Regency into the growing French Empire lay a tangled skein of circumstances—circumstances which underscore the classical tragedy implicit in the fall of the well-guarded city. The most important strand in the skein involved the changing relationship of France and Algiers. The change in this relationship may be measured by two pieces of correspondence. In 1581, Malherbe, secretary to Henri d'Angoulême, the Duke of Provence, wrote to Cafer Pasha, "You will render me a great service and I in turn shall hold myself under obligation to you if you should at any time require assistance of me." The "service rendered" was a request for Algerine intervention to return to French justice one Loys Viguier, who had been advanced 448 *écus* by Marseille merchants for his trip to Constantinople aboard their bark, *La Françoise.* Viguier had absconded to Tripoli while en route.

Some two hundred and fifty years later another Frenchman, Collet, commander of the French naval squadron sent to Algiers in 1827 by Charles X following the fly-whisk incident, handed the following ultimatum to the ruler of Algiers: "His Majesty angered at the horrible and scandalous outrage committed against Himself . . . demands an immediate reparation and public satisfaction prescribed as follows— a public apology, . . . the flag of France will be flown above the forts of Algiers and the Palace of the Dey and shall receive a one-hundred-gun salute."

This French change in attitude from supplicant to blusterer capped a period of contacts between the corsair state and the heartland of European civilization longer than any other in the history of Algiers. France maintained consuls or deputies in the corsair capital continuously from 1579 until 1827. The first formal treaty between the two powers was signed in 1619; it was followed by numerous others, the majority of them dealing with economic concessions and commerce. Even earlier, vessels from Marseille were accustomed to extract coral from the North African coastal reefs in the latter part of the fifteenth century. The slow process of unification of France under the kings of Paris had its effect on Franco-Algerine relations in the growth of representations and complaints on both sides concerning prisoners and interference with naval activities regarded by each as legitimate. Far more than their European rivals, such as Holland and England, the French seized Algerine corsairs for the manpower which could be added to their own galleys. It is worth noting that Algiers had as much trouble in securing the release of its citizens as the French had with theirs—captured corsairs were in most cases assigned to the oars and often simply disappeared!

Provisioning of Algerine vessels was standard practice along the coast of Provence. In 1543 Kheireddin called at Marseille with a fleet of 110 galleys and 40 *fuste*, galliots, and other Mediterranean vessels. The Ottoman admiral was received with due honors by the councilors, invited to the castle for dinner, and provided with powder, shot, and naval stores. The openness of merchants in such Provençal ports nondelivery of their compatriots detained in France and had retaliated with the wholesale seizure of French prizes, twenty in the month of November, 1681, alone, among them a royal frigate carrying the king's envoy on a mission to Italy; he was sold to the principal reis for 11,200 *douros*.

The French armada, commanded by the Marquis Duquesne, moored in Algiers harbor in June, 1683. Duquesne sent a tersely worded memorandum to Baba Hassan, who had succeeded his father-in-law as dey, demanding the release not only of all French but also all Christian prisoners in the city. When the dey failed to reply, Duquesne ordered a bombardment which wreaked considerable damage. The Algerines asked for an armistice and agreed to the release of prisoners, and 570 captives were brought on board the French ships, accompanied by several hostages demanded by Duquesne as security for the truce. One of them was Hűseyin Reis, chief of the *taife*, who earned his nickname Mezamorta —messomorto, "half-dead"—on this occasion because his ship had been fire bombed by one of the French frigates and himself left for dead on its deck, only to revive after the armistice.

Mezamorta convinced Duquesne that if set ashore he could bring about peace, saying, "I can do more in one hour than Baba Hassan in fifteen days." Once at liberty, he was acclaimed by the soldiery with something of the awe accorded a marabout. He seized power, strangled the dey, and set about reorganizing the city's defenses. Hostilities resumed, and after a month of intermittent batterings an enraged crowd went to the French Consulate and sacked it. Blaming Le Vacher for their misfortunes, they took him and twenty other French residents of Algiers, placed each in turn before the mouth of a cannon with his back toward the sea, and as Toulon and Nice spared this coast the horrors visited by the corsairs elsewhere. In the case of Algiers, the friendship with Marseille developed in the latter part of the sixteenth century into the "Africa Concessions" of the Compagnie Lenche, the main French commercial enterprise in Africa before the nineteenth century.

In 1561 a Marseille merchant named Thomas Lenche, originally from Corsica, and one Carlin Didier obtained from Sultan Selim II a firman granting the two a concession for the exclusive right to fish for coral along the North African coast from El Kala, Collo, Bona, and Cape Roux to the mouth of the Oued Seybouse, and to erect forts, batteries, and establishments necessary to the protection and pursuance of this concession. Such was the origin of the trading post which came to be called in time the Bastion of France. The exploitation, to be carried on by Provençal fishermen in accordance with an immemorial custom, confirmed in the Marseillais view a right recognized by Selim I in 1518 after the conquest of Egypt and codified by Article 12 of the Capitulations.

Various vicissitudes afflicted the enterprise and in 1604 the Bastion was burned to the ground by the Turkish garrison at Bona, partly because of the threat represented to the coastal economy and partly in reprisal for Algerines taken by French corsairs active in the area. In 1619 a new concession was negotiated with the Ottomans by the French ambassador to Constantinople. However, the Divan of Algiers refused to restore the Bastion to French control or to return the surviving members of the former French garrison, angry at what they considered a surrender of their patrimony to infidels. "You see what misfortunes are brought upon us by such traders of horses and wheat," Consul Chaix wrote to the City Council of Marseille. "The Divan being angry prepares eighty warships with six thousand men to ravage the whole coast of Provence, and I have run great risk to speak of this subject before it both for myself and for the poor Frenchmen who are here."

Fortunately for the concession, Louis XIII sent to Constantinople in 1623 Captain Sanson Napollon, another Corsican, who had become thoroughly habituated to Ottoman ways as French consul in Aleppo. The mission was concerned equally to recover the Bastion and to encourage Sultan Mustafa I to tighten the reins on the corsairs. Mustafa sent a guard of six *Kapicis* (special messengers) with Napollon, each armed with separate orders, plus thirty letters of instruction, for the authorities in the corsair capital. Napollon also brought 15,000 livres' worth of presents for the Divan, along with a number of Algerine prisoners of war and the two brass cannon taken by Simon Danser on his flight to Marseille some years before. Thus he was able to renegotiate the concession and to win from the sultan the right to restore the Bastion as a protection against the dissident Kabyles of the region, not to mention further reprisals from the Turks. The ransom of Franch prisoners was managed at 200 livres each. Hűseyin Pasha's letter to the Duc de Guise concludes:

Peace being made, there will be sent to you on the part of the victorious Divan one of our most capable officers, and we trust the favor will be returned with an equally accomplished man on your side as Consul. Our peace shall be as that between brothers. . . . It will be expressly forbidden to

*our captains on their corsair campaigns, should they meet
with French vessels, to molest them....*

The implicit surrender of Algerine sovereignty over the
Bastion was assuaged considerably by a contract between the
Divan and Napollon in de Guise's name which specified an
annual payment of 18,00 livres, part to the *ocaḳ* and part to
the state treasury.

The peace so laboriously established was observed more
conscientiously by the Algerines than by the French, although the independent atttiude of the corsairs and the inability of the French fleet to patrol the Mediterranean coast
made implementation difficult on both sides. Sanson Napollon's death in 1633 during an abortive attempt to seize
the island of Tabarka, off the Tunisian coast near the town
of the same name, as an observation post for the Bastion,
deprived the Algerines of one of the few Christian leaders
whom they trusted. The Divan became particularly incensed
over periodic ruptures of their peace by individual French
captains. One of these, Roger de Castellux, after having been
sheltered in Algiers harbor under a flag of truce and given
provisions and fresh bread, sailed away under a flag of war,
intercepted two Algerine merchant ships from Tunis, and
took them as prizes with seventy prisoners to Toulon. Actions
such as this one led the Divan to order the destruction of the
Bastion for the second time; its population of 317 French
were taken to Algiers as captives and the Algerines swore
they would not allow a renewal of the agreement between
themselves and Napollon by virtue of the bad faith demon-
strated by France.

As the seventeenth century progressed, France and Algiers

came increasingly on a collision course, prompted by the withdrawal of the corsair guild from intervention in the internal affairs of the Regency in favor of the military regime of the deys and the centralization of French power under the Sun King and his successor. A favorite tactic of French captains was to cast anchor in Algiers harbor near enough to encourage Christian prisoners working at the docks or arsenal to make a break for freedom by swimming out to the waiting ships.

In 1673 Dey Haci Mohammed wrote to Louis XIV to complain bitterly of a certain Captain d'Almeras, who had brought eight vessels into the harbor in August and anchored inside normal range of the batteries; forty-six prisoners made their break, and as soon as they were aboard d'Almeras weighed anchor and sailed away. The dey observed in the same correspondence that Frenchmen were to be found frequently "in the ships of our enemies, such as Genoa, Portugal, Spain, Holland and Malta, where they fight against our people and kill them;" that Turks escaping from imprisonment in countries with whom Algiers was at war, and "taking refuge in your kingdom because of the peace which exists between us, are made slaves and sent to the galleys." He added that the theft of captives caused him much personal distress as "I am then confronted by their enraged owners." As Hussein Dey was to do in 1827, Haci Mohammed observed somewhat plaintively, "We have now written you two or three letters without reply, and when this one shall reach your presence, inform us with all possible speed as to what your intentions are, in order that we may take proper measures and that we know if you desire to live at peace with us or not."

During the tenure of Consul Jean Le Vacher, apostolic vicar of the Jesuit Order, in Algiers occurred the most significant sequence of events affecting Franco-Algerine relations until those of 1827–30. Le Vacher undertook a serious effort to ransom all French captives in the corsair capital and for humanitarian reasons pressed for the concurrent return of Algerines, "whether Turks or Moors," held prisoner in France. In 1676 he obtained the release of twenty-one French sailors, who were repatriated on the bark *Ste-Anne–St.-Joseph*, against twenty-two Turks brought to Algiers on the same boat. His costs for this effort included "seventy pounds eight sous 3 deniers" incurred for the provisioning of the aforesaid vessel and paid out of his own pocket.

Le Vacher's further efforts in this direction led to more unfortunate, if not disastrous, results. In 1681 he wrote the Marseille city council to advise that the Divan "awaited with impatience the repatriation of all Turks and Moors still held in France," since they had agreed to the same exchange procedure as before, and he urged the sending of Hayet, the royal commandant of Marine, to Algiers with an attestation in Turkish signed by the leading Turks held in Marseille to the effect that by royal order all captives had been removed from the galleys and their movements in the French city were not restricted. A year later Le Vacher wrote to inquire as to what was happening between France and Algiers, he having had no response to his requests and no news of peace or war.

What was happening was a move toward war. An earlier French bombardment of Algiers in 1660 had produced no results. The French now prepared a second armada, on the ground that the corsairs had begun to attack French ships. In fact, the Algerines had declared the peace broken by the nondelivery of their compatriots detained in France and had retaliated with the wholesale seizure of French prizes, twenty in the month of November, 1681, alone, among them a royal frigate carrying the king's envoy on a mission to Italy; he was sold to the principal reis for 11,200 *douros*.

The French armada, commanded by the Marquis Duquesne, moored in Algiers harbor in June, 1683. Duquesne sent a tersely worded memorandum to Baba Hassan, who had succeeded his father-in-law as dey, demanding the release not only of all French but also all Christian prisoners in the city. When the dey failed to reply, Duquesne ordered a bombardment which wreaked considerable damage. The Algerines asked for an armistice and agreed to the release of prisoners, and 570 captives were brought on board the French ships, accompanied by several hostages demanded by Duquesne as security for the truce. One of them was Hűseyin Reis, chief of the *taife*, who earned his nickname Mezamorta —messomorto, "half-dead"—on this occasion because his ship had been fire bombed by one of the French frigates and himself left for dead on its deck, only to revive after the armistice.

Mezamorta convinced Duquesne that if set ashore he could bring about peace, saying, "I can do more in one hour than Baba Hassan in fifteen days." Once at liberty, he was acclaimed by the soldiery with something of the awe accorded a marabout. He seized power, strangled the dey, and set about reorganizing the city's defenses. Hostilities resumed, and after a month of intermittent batterings an enraged crowd went to the French Consulate and sacked it. Blaming Le Vacher for their misfortunes, they took him and twenty other French residents of Algiers, placed each in turn before the mouth of a cannon with his back toward the sea, and blew them in the general direction of the invasion fleet. From then on this particular cannon was called by the Algerines "the Consular"; in 1830 it was brought to Brest, where it has since adorned the entrance to that port. The incident confirmed the intransigence of both sides, and Mezamorta on his part affirmed that he would be willing to make peace, but under no circumstances would he deal with Duquesne, whom he called "a man without words." Duquesne was finally replaced by de Tourville, who negotiated in April, 1684, a "Hundred-Year Peace."

As the respect accorded him by the Porte would indicate, the new dey proved an effective ruler of Algiers. He also kept the peace, and there was considerable traffic in prisoners between France and Algiers, sometimes accompanied by rich presents. The Marquis d'Amfreville in conveying one group of Algerines to be repatriated brought with him the dey's envoy, Haci Cafer, who had received as parting gifts from the king three muskets, three pistolets, a saber encrusted with gems, rich cloths and brocades, a six-pendulum clock, twelve gold medals, six tapestries, and an eight-branched candelabra. Hüseyin responded with a gift of twelve of the finest Barbary horses.

However, differences of opinion concerning the Bastion of France, and the belief of the Algerines that its French governor was meddling in their affairs and intriguing with the Kabyles against the garrison in Bona, brought a warning from the Divan against such interference. The French responded with another expedition, commanded by Marshal d'Estrées, which arrived before Algiers in June, 1688, with a complement of forty-one ships, displayed warning signals on a raft which was sent into the inner harbor, and then commenced a bombardment lasting through the first half of July. Some eight hundred houses were destroyed and the city's mosques and walls suffered considerable damage. Mezamorta agreed to sign a new peace treaty, an action which angered the *ocak* to the point of rebellion, and the dey left Algiers quickly for Tunis, from where he traveled to Constantinople to take up the position promised him by the sultan.

The expedition of d'Estrées had no more positive results than any of its predecessors, and the stabilization of Regency government itself in the eighteenth century—the average length of an eighteenth-century dey's rule was seven years—introduced a certain regularity into French-Algerine relations. To a large extent complaints regarding violations of the peace were resolved through direct correspondence between the two chiefs of state. When, for example, a corsair ship which normally carried repatriated prisoners to and from Algiers was seized by a French privateer while en route to Oran to purchase wheat for the Regency and towed into port at Toulon, the dey made his demand for restitution directly to the king. On their part, the Algerines generally observed the ancient tradition which forbade them to take prizes within thirty miles of the coast of Provence, the region dependent on Marseille; when they violated this tradition—as in the taking of a Genoese bark off Bandol in 1728— it was for reasons of war which compelled them to refuse the request of the Porte itself for restitution. As the dey explained, "Authority in the Regency is in the hands of the Divan and *ocak*; only they can make a determination."

The war between France and Tunis in 1711–12 caused difficulties for the French with Algiers mainly because of failure to distinguish between the vessels of the two regencies. An Algerian xebec was captured off Toulon, and as a consequence the Algerine authorities detained the managers of the Compagnie d'Afrique (successor to the Compagnie Lenche) in Bona and El Kala and padlocked the company's warehouses. The French action in sending prompt payment to Algiers for the shipwreck of a bark from Martigues in which several Algerine merchants had taken passage to Turkey and were lost with all their cargoes and effects, eased the situation. However the Regency continued to object to the practice of issuing French passports to citizens of Genoa and other Christian enemies of Algiers, to protect their vessels and persons from seizure by the corsairs.

Another sore point was the requirement imposed by the Algerines that no one be permitted in the presence of the dey bearing arms. Consul Leon Delane (1731–32) angrily refused to deposit his sword outside the audience chamber, claiming it was beneath his dignity and rights as a "Consul, a Chevalier de Saint-Lazare, and an officer of the King" to submit to the requirement. The same consul, who had previously served as French consul in Candia (Crete) and had caused much trouble by his haughtiness and scorn for the Turks, interfered with the attempt by a sailor from St. Tropez to turn renegade, although the treaty between the two states specifically stated (Article 19) that if a Frenchman persisted for three consecutive days in his intention to turn Muslim he should be so recognized. Eventually Delane was reassigned to Candia, and his replacement, Benoit Lemaire, left his sword outside the audience chamber, whereupon the dey granted him the right to wear it within.

Rivalries between France and England, and with other

European nations engaged in the growing struggle for domination of the continent and the later contest for colonial possessions, involved Algiers largely through the persons of their respective consuls. The English in particular enjoyed some advantage, as the personalities of the French envoys were often ill suited to dealings with the rather intractable and frequently haughty Turks. The consuls of France made frequent representations to the deys and to their own government concerning the intrigues of their English rivals. Thus in 1733 the Comte de Maurepas, minister of the Marine, warned Dey Ibrahim not to listen to the "seductive propositions of the English" to aid Algiers in driving the Spanish from Oran, in return for commercial privileges, and pointed out to Ibrahim that by acceptance he would exchange a weak neighbor (Spain) for a powerful one, England. The dey was unimpressed, and in reply ordered the replacement of French Consul Lemaire as the source of the intrigue.

Dey Baba Mohammed, who in his correspondence referred regularly to "Algiers, the site of continual combat against the infidels," along with equally warm protestations of friendship for France, died on July 12, 1791, at the advanced age of eighty-one, after a tranquil reign of twenty-four years. He was succeeded by his adopted son Hassan, who immediately ratified the existing treaties of friendship and commerce with France. Louis XVI sent his congratulations to the new dey in September and noted with satisfaction the decision to send an envoy to the sultan in Constantinople aboard a French vessel to obtain the caftan of investiture from Selim III. Hassan informed him that, "it being the obligation of new Deys to send such an embassy and presents to the Sublime Porte," he had requested the use of a French

vessel "being the safest and most highly esteemed" for transportation. It was to be the last communication between royalty
in France and Algiers. In 1792 the French monarchy fell,
setting in motion a new train of circumstances under which
the recognition accorded the French Republic by the Regency
would in time generate the downfall of the corsair state.

The French Revolution found the Regency well disposed
toward the Republic at the start. Citizen Gaspard Monge,
who became later president of the French Institute at Cairo
and a senator, advised Hassan of his assumption of authority
over French maritime interests as minister of Marine, and in
that capacity prevailed upon the Republic of Genoa to return
two Algerian xebecs seized in French waters and conveyed
to Toulon. Hassan in turn notified the French Republic of
his intention to honor existing Franco-Algerine treaties and
agreed to the continuation of Consul Philippe Vallière at his
post. The Committee of Public Safety proceeded with an
inquiry as to the neutrality of the three regencies, having
scented that war with the coalition was not far off.

The support rendered to a French vessel attacked by a
Spanish frigate within sight of Algiers by the corsairs in
April, 1795, was noted with much satisfaction as proof of the
harmony prevailing between France and the Regency. Two
days before the sixth anniversary of Bastille Day, the dey
wrote the Committee to recommend particularly the services
of Jacob Cohen Bacri, a Jew from Marseille whose father,
Michel (originally from Livorno), had established some years
earlier an export-import business in Algiers and had won the
confidence of officials of the Regency. Michel Bacri's firm had
already advanced on credit some two million tons of wheat
to the municipalities, the fleet, and the armies of France.

The younger Bacri's representative in Algiers was Nephtali
Busnach, while another Jew, Simon Abucaya, maintained
for the firm an office in Paris, where he called himself "General Agent of the Dey of Algiers." The dey's confidence in
France at that time was such that he agreed to loan the
Republic 200,000 Spanish piasters, for two years at no interest,
from the Regency treasury to pay the costs of its consular and
commercial establishments in Algiers.

During 1796 and 1797, contingent with the rise of Bona-
parte and the extension of France's wars with her European
rivals, Busnach and Bacri continued to provide wheat to the
French armies, while their representative in Paris continued
to press for payment. The new French consul in Algiers, Saint-
André, advised his superiors not to make payment until it
was clear that the influence of "these Jews over the mind of
Sidi Hassan" would not prejudice French interests in the
Regency in favor of the British. At the same time Saint-
André reported to the dey that Bonaparte's victories, his
chastisement of Venice, and the release of Muslim prisoners
in Genoa, Livorno, Zante, and Corfu were conclusive proof
of the good intentions and continued friendship of the Republic for Algiers.

But it was not to be. The deys continued to press their
demands for payment on behalf of Busnach and Bacri, of
whom they were in fact patrons, and the Directory continued
to evade its responsibility. Among other reasons, it claimed
that the two entrepreneurs were provisioning the English at
Gibraltar at the same time. In 1798, on the eve of the French
expedition to Egypt, Talleyrand was instructed to receive
Abucaya and to accept the obligation owing to the Bacris.
The representative of the firm presented a bill for 2,297,415

francs, emphasizing the firm's long-term unpaid services to France. The French, who feared that the coming expedition might provoke the Algerines to interfere with its passage across the Mediterranean, agreed to pay 170,000 livres bi-weekly until the debt had been liquidated. War with the Ottoman Empire aborted the commitment; on at least this occasion the Algerine fidelity to the Porte worked against its interests.

Shortly after Bonaparte's landing in Egypt, Selim III sent a firman to Algiers along with the caftan of investiture for the new dey, Mustafa (1798–1805) ordering the Regency to declare war against France. At first the Algerines de-murred, but the arrival of a second messenger from the Porte with further orders forced them to move. They were en-couraged by the warning of Selim's envoy that failure to obey would be regarded as treason; the Ottoman fleet would then join the English squadron of Admiral Keith to come and chastise Algiers. The French reacted to the declaration of war and the imprisonment of their consul with a sequestra-tion of the property of Bacri and his agent in Paris. Peace was re-established in 1802 as a consequence of the Treaty of Amiens. Napoleon spoke vaguely of an expedition against Algiers—in the Secret Treaty of Tilsit (1807) between him and Alexander of Russia, Article 5 stated that "the cities of Africa, such as Tunis, Algiers, will be occupied by the French and at the general peace will be given in indemnity to the kings of Sicily and Sardinia." But he took no serious steps; the conquest of the three-hundred-year-old corsair state was left to other hands.

By 1805 the debt owed to Busnach and Bacri had grown to 8,154,012 francs 51 centimes. The government in Algiers changed, with Akhmed (*var.*) replacing Mustafa as dey, but the demands and recriminations continued, as each dey sought to obtain not only what was due the Jewish entrepreneurs but also his proper share as patron and backer. France paid Bacri on account 1,200,000 francs, placed on deposit in Marseille, refusing to pay more. In 1819 a European flotilla commanded jointly by English Admiral Fremantle and French Admiral Jurien de La Gravière called at Algiers and presented a demand "by the United Powers of Europe" addressed to the dey only as "Prince" that Algiers subscribe to the agreement to outlaw maritime piracy signed at the Congress of Aix-la-Chapelle. It was the sole collaborative European effort against the Regency in its entire history.

Hussein, who was a reasonable man, replied that he would continue to treat his enemies as enemies, and his friends as friends; he saw a great difference between the practice of his nation and the highway robbery of the French in refusing to honor a just debt. "If one of my subjects owed money to the King of France," he told Consul Jacques Deval, "justice would be done within twenty-four hours." He began to suspect France of bad faith. He also suspected that Deval, whose long residence in Ottoman territories—his father was a dragoman at the Porte—had added a healthy dislike of the Turks to his native arrogance, was intriguing against him. His suspicions hardened when the consul accused him of deceit in the seizure of two vessels belonging to the pope by Algerine corsairs, who had taken them to Bona and sold them, the Papal States having no treaty relations with Algiers and paying no tribute.

On April 30, 1827, in accordance with long-established tradition, Deval went to felicitate the dey on the occasion of the Grand Bayram which followed the end of Ramadan. What actually transpired on that occasion is in dispute, but the shoulder tap with an embroidered fly whisk which Hussein gave the consul as a signal to end their interview was interpreted as an insult to the person, and the honor, of France. For the next three years the French fleet maintained a desultory blockade of Algiers, while the Porte endeavored to mediate in the dispute. Sultan Mahmud II feared the loss of Ottoman territory, but the dey, confident that the powers which had always protected Algiers would continue to do so, held to his position.

Mahmud's attempts at mediation were ignored, as were his warnings to the Algerine government in firman after firman that its refusal to settle the dispute with France would have serious consequences. In March, 1830, the sultan made one last attempt. He named Halil, the former grand mufti of Algiers, living then in retirement in Izmir, to proceed to the corsair capital and obtain "peace before war" between the dey and France. Mahmud's orders to the former mufti stated *inter alia*, "I have informed the French Ambassador to Constantinople of your assignment, since Algiers is under my rule and there is peace between my state and his which will continue forever." The envoy was ordered to convince the Algerines to obey the sultan's wishes in token of their fealty, and thereafter to mediate in face-to-face talks. Unfortunately, by the time he reached Tunis it was too late, and the Tunisians as noted earlier would not permit him to proceed to Algiers.

Thus the Regency of Algiers disappeared from the roster of Mediterranean states as swiftly and completely as it had arisen. It had been born in a violent age and it died in another, the difference being that the brutality of the second was economic and exploitative rather than religious. The fall of Algiers, more positively than the fall of Egypt to Napoleon's Army of the East, opened the floodgates for European colonization of Africa. For three centuries corsair Algiers had stood as a powerful obstacle to European intervention, and in the process had stamped a definite Turkish design, a distinctive pattern originally from the East, on the western Mediterranean. The watchtowers of the Spanish, Italian, and French coasts guard a peaceful landscape today, but their crumbling stonework attests to the long period when the Algerine corsair was the mightiest figure of his age.

SELECTED BIBLIOGRAPHY

The full story of corsair Algiers can only be told through
the piecing together of a great variety of sources, and a proper
assessment of its role in Mediterranean history has required
a re-examination of known materials whose relationship to
each other was not established previously because of their
cultural, linguistic, or political diversity. Chronicles of the
Algerine state, if they ever existed, have disappeared. There
seems not to have been any official position such as that of
archivist within the Algerine administration. The Ottoman
historians and court record keepers, perhaps because of the
independent posture and remoteness of Algiers, took note of
the state in principle when its contributions advanced specific
Ottoman interests and otherwise infrequently. Consequently,

much bibliographical work remains to be done on Algiers. Good firsthand accounts of Algerine life were kept by European observers, travelers, and resident representatives of Christian Mediterranean states in the corsair capital.

The basic bibliographical reference remains Sir Robert L. Playfair, *A Bibliography of Algeria from the Expedition of Charles V in 1541 to 1887* (Bibliography of the Barbary States series, Royal Geographical Society *Supplementary Papers*, Vol. I, London, William Clowes & Son, 1889). The bibliography in C.-A. Julien, *History of North Africa: Tunisia, Algeria, Morocco* (English ed., translated by John Petrie; New York, Praeger, 1970; originally published as *Histoire de l'Afrique du Nord*; Paris, Payot, 1952), is extensive but omits entirely the Turkish and to a large extent the Spanish, English, and Italian sources. The only full-scale scholarly study in Turkish of the Ottomans in North Africa to date is Aziz Samih İlter, *Şimali Afrikáda Türkler* (2 vols.; Istanbul, 1937), which draws on Ottoman archival materials, but includes little social or economic history. The handful of Turkish secondary sources, such as Fuad Carim, *Cezayir'de Türkler* (Istanbul, Sanat Basimevi, 1962), draw heavily on İlter or else reiterate material from the standard European sources on Algiers.

Materials for the study of corsair Algiers fall into four general classifications: archival collections, treaties and documents, primary sources, and secondary sources, the great majority of these last being drawn from primary accounts with little or no interpretation. In addition, certain journals, notably *Revue Africaine*, published by the Société Historique Algeriénne in Algiers from 1856 to 1962, contain a wealth of material translated by French scholars from the original

Arabic or Turkish documents during the period of French rule in Algeria. A complete collection of this valuable journal is maintained in the Archives d'Outre-Mer at the Université d'Aix-Marseille, Aix-en-Provence, France.

Archival Collections

Archives Communales de Toulon. Series, *Archives du Port.* See especially CC. 523.

Archives Departmentales du Bouches-du-Rhone, Fonds Jaubert. Series 357 E, Register 36, Series 390 E, Register 58, F. 987.

Archives Historiques de la Chambre de Commerce de Marseille. AA Series, *Origines du Consulat de la Nation Française à Alger*; J Series, Nos. 1338–1400, *Correspondance dés Consuls, Comptes de la Nation Française, Actes de Catholicité.* . . . *Cf.* Octave Teissier, *Inventaire des Archives Historiques . . . Marseille.* Marseille, Société Historique, 1939.

Archivos de Simancas, Simancas (Salamanca), Valladolid, Spain (sometimes refered to as Archivos Generales de Espana). Eighteen miscellaneous folders on Hispano-Algerine relations (accounts of captivity, expeditions, armaments, and so on). *Cf.* D. Angel de la Playa Boros. *Inventario et Guia del Investigador.* Madrid; Sociedad de Bibliofilos Españoles, 1962.

Başbakanlīk Arşivi (formerly Başvekâlet Arşivi)—Archives of the Office of the Prime Minister—Istanbul. The principal repository of communications between the Ottoman Porte and the *ocak* is the series *Defterler-i-Ahkam-i-Mühimme-i-Divan-i-Humayun* (Register of important decrees of the Imperial Divan), usually abbreviated *Mühimme defterleri.*

Hariciye Vekâleti (Archives of the Ottoman Foreign Ministry), Istanbul. These records, housed along with the above ones within the complex of buildings formerly known as the Sublime Porte, contain some correspondence between the Porte and European powers relative to Algiers. Some of the documents are in the original language, and some are copies of European communications translated into Osmanli Turkish. Of interest is Dosya 708, *Cezayir'in Fransa Tarafindan işgali Mesail-i siyasiye* (Diplomatic Problems relative to the Occupation by France of Algiers).

Topkapī Sarayi Müzesi Arşivi (Archives of the Museum of Topkapi Palace), Istanbul, have a few references to Algiers in Series E., Nos. 5136, 5148, 3584, and 3454.

Some additional archival material may be found in the collection *Acta Turcorum*, Drzavni Archivu Dubrovniku (State Archives of Dubrovnik), Dubrovnik, Yugoslavia, formerly known as the Republic of Ragusa; the Archives of the Jewish Nation, preserved in Leghorn, Italy; the Archives of the Regency of Tunis, housed in the Ministry of Foreign Affairs, Republic of Tunisia (in Tunis); and the Real Academia, Madrid, Spain.

Treaty Collections, Documents

Charrière, Ernest, comp. *Negociations de la France dans le Levant* . . . . 4 vols. Paris, Imprimerie Nationale, 1848–60. Vol. I deals with Algiers.

Harris, William, ed. *A Complete Collection of Treaties Subsisting between Great Britain and France, Spain, Algiers*

. . . 1456–1763. London, J. Steele and J. Millan, 1779. See Vol. XVI, Nos. iii and xxiii.

Hertslet, Lewis, comp. *Hertslet's Commercial Treaties.* 31 vols. London, Henry Butterworth, 1835–. Of particular interest are Vol. I, *Treaties of Peace and Commerce, Algiers*; Vol. III, *Declarations Respecting Algiers*; Vol. V, *Act of Parliament Respecting British Sovereignty.* England recognized French sovereignty over Algeria on May 30, 1837.

Mas-Latrie, Louis de., ed. *Traités de Paix et de Commerce et Documents Divers concernant les relations des Chrétiens avec les Arabes de l'Afrique du Nord.* . . . 2 vols. Paris, Plon, 1866; *Supplément.* Paris: J. Baur, 1872.

Nouradounghian, Gabriel, comp. *Recueil d' Actes Internationaux de l'Empire Ottomane.* Paris, Librairie Cotillon, 1900.

Plantet, Eugene. *La Correspondance des Deys d'Alger avec la Cour de France, 1597–1833,* 2 vols. Paris, 1898. An invaluable documentary record with extensive explanatory footnotes for the correspondence.

Testa, Baron I. de. *Recueil des Traités de la Porte Ottomane avec les Puissances Étrangères.* Paris, Chez les Auteurs, 1898.

Primary Sources

Aranda, Emmanuel. *Relation de la Captivité et Liberté du Sieur Emmanuel d'Aranda.* Paris, 1696. Original published in Spanish, Madrid: 1642. English edition, London, 1666.

d'Arvieux, Le Chevalier. *Memoires du Chevalier d'Arvieux.* . . . Ed. by R. P. Jean-Baptiste Labat. 6 vols. Paris, 1735.

Esp. Vol. V. D'Arvieux was French consul in Algiers, 1674–80.

Broughton, Elizabeth. *Six Years Residence in Algiers, 1806–1812.* London, Saunders & Otley, 1840. A diary of the author's mother combined with personal childhood reminiscences.

Dalrymple, Major William. *Travels through Spain and Portugal with a Short Account of the Spanish Expedition against Algiers in 1775.* London, J. Almon, 1777.

Dan, Rev. Père. *Histoire de Barbarie et ses Corsars, des Royaumes et des Villes d'Alger.* Paris: 1637; 2d ed., 1649. Dutch translation by G. Brockhuijsen. Amsterdam, 1648.

Davies, William. *A True Relation of the Travels & Most Miserable Captivity of William Davies, Barber-Surgeon of London, under the Duke of Livorno* . . . London, 1614. Chapter II deals with "Argier" [*sic*].

Foss, John. *Journal of the Captivity and Sufferings of John Foss, Several Years a Prisoner in Algiers.* Newburyport, Mass., 1797.

Galan, Diego. *Cautiverio y Trabajos de Diego Galan.* Madrid, Sociedad de Bibliofilos Españoles, 1913.

Gramaye (or Grammaye or Grammey), Sieur Jean-Baptiste. *Les Cruautés exercées sur les Chrétiens en la Ville d' Argier en Barbarie.* Paris: 1620. English version in Samuel Purchas, *Purchas His Pilgrimage, or Nations of the World* . . . *Observed.* Vol. II. 5 books (4 vols.).

Haedo, Fray Diego de. *Topographia e Historia General de Argel.* Valladolid, Spain: 1612. French translation published in *Revue Africaine*, 1870. Republished by the So-

ciedad de Bibliofilos Españoles in 3 vols. Madrid, 1927–29.
———. *Epitome de los Reyes de Argel.* Valladolid, 1612. The two books by Haedo contain almost all that is known of sixteenth-century Algiers.

Laugier de Tassy, N. *Histoire du Royaume d'Alger avec l'etat présent de son gouvernement.* Amsterdam, 1725. The author was commissioner of Marine for the king of Spain in Holland and visited Algiers in 1685.

Losada, Fr. Gabriel Gomez. *Escuela de Trabajos.* 4 vols. Madrid, 1670. See Vol. II, *Noticias y gobierno de Argel.*
———. *Con la Vida del Martyr Pedro Pascual de Valencia.* Madrid, 1670.

Marana, Jean Paul. *Dialogo fra Genova et Algieri, città fulminate dal Giove Gallico.* Amsterdam, 1685. French translation issued in the same year as *Dialogue de Gènes et Alger....*

Marmol-Carvajal, L. *Descripcion General de Affrica. ...* 3 vols. Granada, Spain: 1573–99; French translation by Pierre d'Ablancourt. *L'Afrique de Marmol.* 3 vols. Paris, 1867.

Morgan, Joseph. *A Compleat History of the Present Seat of War in Africa ... with a new Map of the Kingdom of Algiers.* London: 1732. The same author's *History of Algiers* (London, 1728) is a pirated version of Laugier de Tassy (*q.v.*).

Nicolay, Nicolas de. *The Peregrinations & Voyages Made Into Turkie....* Translated by T. Washington the younger. London, Thomas Dawson, 1585. Also in Purchas, Vol. II.

Noah, Mordecai M. *Travels in England, France, Spain and the Barbary States.* New York, 1819. Contains the text of the "Treaty of Peace & Amity between the United States and Algiers" of September 5, 1795, ratified by the Senate March 2, 1796.

Pananti, Pilippo. *Avventura e osservasioni sopra la costa di Barberia.* 2 vols. Florence: 1817. English translation by Edward Blaquier. *Narrative of a Residence in Algiers....* London, 1818.

Pitts, Joseph. *A True and Faithful Account of the Religion and Manners of the Mahometans ... Algiers.* London, 1738.

Rang, Sander and Ferdinand Denis. *Fondation de la Regence d'Alger; Histoire des Barberousses* (translation of the sixteenth-century Arabic manuscript *Ghazawat 'Aruj wa Khair al-Din*). 2 vols. Paris, 1837.

Rousseau, Alphonse. *Chronique de la Régence d'Alger* (translation of al-Gaylani, *al-Zohrat al-Nayarat*). Algiers, 1841.

Salame, A. *A Narrative of the Expedition to Algiers under the Command of the Right Hon. Viscount Exmouth.* London: 1819. The author accompanied the expedition as official interpreter.

Shaler, William. *Sketches of Algiers.* Boston, Century, 1826. The author was United States consul to Algiers until 1826. The book contains an eyewitness report of the Exmouth attack and a consular journal kept during the year 1823.

Shaw, Rev. Thomas. *Travels and Observations Relating to Several parts of Barbary and the Levant.* Oxford, 1738.

Tyler, Royall. *The Algerine Captive, or the Life & Adventures of Doctor Updike Underhill, Six Years a Prisoner in Algiers.* Walpole, N. H.: D. Carlisle, 1797. Reissued with an Introduction by Jack B. Moore. Gainesville, Fla., Scholars Facsimiles and Reprints, 1967. Although ostensibly fictional, this work by one of America's earliest writers contains a great deal of first-hand information about the corsair state. The dedication is to David Humphreys, who as United States minister plenipotentiary to Lisbon was charged with prisoner release negotiations with the Algerines.

Secondary Sources

Abun Nasr, Jamil. *History of the Maghrib*. Cambridge, Cambridge University Press, 1971.

Bono, Salvatore. *I Corsari Barbareschi*. Turin, 1964.

Boyer, Pierre. *La Vie Quotidienne à Alger à la Veille de l'Intervention Française*. Paris, Hachette, 1963.

Bradford, Ernle. *The Sultan's Admiral*. New York, Harcourt, Brace & World, 1968. Account of the life of Kheireddin.

————. *Mediterranean: Portrait of a Sea*. London, Hodder & Stroughton, 1971. Has a chapter on the corsairs.

Esterhazy, Walsin. *De la Domination Turque dans l'ancienne Régence d'Alger*. Paris, Charles Gosselin, 1840.

Fisher, Geoffrey. *Barbary Legend*. Oxford, Oxford University Press, 1957.

de Grammont, H. D. *Histoire d'Alger sous la domination Turque*. Paris, 1887.

de la Gravière, Jurien. *Les Corsaires Barbaresques et la Marine de Soliman le Grand*. Paris, Plon, 1887.

Hubac, Pierre. *Les Barbaresques*. Paris, Editions Berger-Levrault, 1949.

Masson, Paul. *Histoire des etablissements et du commerce Française dans l'Afrique Barbaresque, 1560–1793*. Paris, 1903.

Mercier, Ernest. *Histoire de l'Afrique Septentrionale depuis les Temps les plus reculés jusqu'à la Conquête Française.* 3 vols. Paris, Leroux, 1891. See in particular Vol. III.

Playfair, R. L. *The Scourge of Christendom: Annals of British Relations with Algiers Prior to the French Conquest.* London, Smith Elder & Co., 1884.

Renaudot, M. *Alger: Tableau du Royaume de la Ville d'Alger.* . . . 4th edition. Paris, Librairie Universelle, 1830.

Russell, Michael. *History and Present Condition of the Barbary States, Comprehending a View of their civil institutions, antiquities, arts, religion, literature, commerce, agricultural and natural production* . . . . Edinburgh, Oliver & Boyd, 1835.

INDEX